P9-CRF-495

Orthodox Perspectives

The Greek Orthodox Theological Review

Volume 30   Summer 1985   Number 2

Published by the

Holy Cross Orthodox Press

for the

Holy Cross Greek Orthodox School of Theology, Hellenic College

Orthodox Perspectives
on Baptism, Eucharist, and Ministry

Edited by: Gennadios Limouris
and Nomikos Michael Vaporis

Faith and Order Papers, Number 128.

Holy Cross Orthodox Press
Brookline, Massachusetts O2146

We are extremely pleased to acknowledge the generosity of His Eminence Archbishop Iakovos who generously provided the funds for the publication of this volume.

Copyright © Holy Cross Orthodox Press, 1985

Published by Holy Cross Orthodox Press
50 Goddard Avenue
Brookline, Massachusetts 02146

All rights reserved. No part of this publication may be reproduced, stored in a retrieval system, or transmitted, in any form or by any means, electronic, mechanical, photocopying, recording or otherwise, without the prior permission of Holy Cross Orthodox Press.

Cover design by Mary C. Vaporis

Library of Congress Cataloging-in-Publication Data
Main entry under title:

Orthodox perspectives on baptism, Eucharist, and ministry.

(WCC faith and order papers; no. 128)
"The studies in this volume first appeared in the Greek Orthodox Theological Review, volume 30, number 2, (1985)"—Verso CIP t.p.
"Papers produced by the Inter-Orthodox Symposium on Baptism, Eucharist, and Ministry held on the campus of Hellenic College/Holy Cross Orthodox School of Theology from 11-18 June 1985"—Editor's pref.
   Bibliography: p.
   1. Baptism, Eucharist and ministry—Congresses. 2. Sacraments and Christian union—Congresses. 3. Baptism—Congresses. 4. Lord's Supper—Congresses. 5. Clergy—Office—Congresses. 6. Orthodox Eastern Church—Doctrines—Congresses. I. Limouris, Gennadios. II. Vaporis, N. M. (Nomikos Michael), 1926—   . III. Inter-Orthodox Symposium on Baptism, Eucharist, and Ministry (1985: Hellenic College) IV. Series: Faith and order paper; 128.
       BX9.5.S2B3636   1985   234'.16   85-27298
           ISBN 0-917651-22-7 (pbk.)

Contents

v

CONTRIBUTORS

Archbishop Iakovos, Primate of the Greek Orthodox Archdiocese of North and South America, Exarch of the Ecumenical Patriarchate.

Metropolitan Dr Antonie of Transylvania, Rumanian Orthodox Church, Member of Central Committee, World Council of Churches.

Bishop Nerses Bozabalian, Armenian Apostolic Church, Etchmiadzin, Member of Central Committee, World Council of Churches.

Rev Dr Emilio Castro, General Secretary, World Council of Churches.

Metropolitan Prof Dr Chrysostomos of Myra, Ecumenical Patriarchate of Constantinople, Vice-Moderator of Central Committee, World Council of Churches.

Rev Dr Günther Gassmann, Evangelical Church in Germany: Lutheran, Director of the Commission on Faith and Order, World Council of Churches, Geneva, Switzerland.

Rev Dr K. M. George, Orthodox Syrian Church of the East, Member of Commission on Faith and Order, World Council of Churches.

Rev Prof Dr Thomas Hopko, St. Vladimir's Seminary, New York, USA, Member of Commission on Faith and Order, World Council of Churches.

Archbishop Kirill of Smolensk, Russian Orthodox Church, Member of Central Committee and Commission on Faith and Order, World Council of Churches.

Rev Dr Gennadios Limouris, Archimandrite, Ecumenical Patriarchate of Constantinople, Executive Secretary, Commission on Faith and Order, World Council of Churches, Geneva, Switzerland.

Prof Nikos Nissiotis, President, Department of Pastoral Theology, University of Athens, former Moderator of Commission on Faith and Order.

Rev Prof Dr Theodore Stylianopoulos, Holy Cross Greek Orthodox School of Theology, Brookline/MA, USA, Member of Central Committee, World Council of Churches.

Editor's Preface

The Greek Orthodox Theological Review is happy and, indeed, honored to publish the papers produced by the Inter-Orthodox Symposium on Baptism, Eucharist, and Ministry held on the campus of Hellenic College/Holy Cross Orthodox School of Theology from 11-18 June 1985.

The gathering of forty-five hierarchs and theologians of the Eastern Orthodox and Oriental Orthodox Churches to discuss the "Lima document" was a very important event for Orthodoxy as well as for the ecumenical movement. *The Greek Orthodox Theological Review* hopes that by publishing the papers of the Symposium, many others not present will be able to benefit from the theological dialogue that took place on the campus of Hellenic College.

At this point it is only proper to thank Archbishop Iakovos, Primate of the Greek Orthodox Archdiocese of North and South America and Exarch of the Ecumenical Patriarchate, for generously providing the funds for the publication of this volume.

The present number of the *Review* is also being published independently as No. 128 in the series: "Faith and Order Papers." This number was co-edited by The Very Reverend Dr Gennadios Limouris, Archimandrite of the Ecumenical Patriarchate and Executive Secretary, Commission on Faith and Order, World Council of Churches.

N. M. Vaporis
Editor

An Address to the Opening Plenary Session

ARCHBISHOP IAKOVOS

Your Eminence, Beloved Brother in Christ, Metropolitan Chrysostomos of Myra,
Fellow Hierarchy,
Honored Members and Participants,
Dear Brothers and Sisters:

IT IS A GREAT PLEASURE for me to be able to welcome and greet you on this Holy Cross campus as you are about to commence your deliberations on the most important document ever produced by the Faith and Order Commission of the World Council of Churches.

The challenge is great, as great is the opportunity to further the historic step taken in Lima, Peru. We, the Orthodox, are not to simply comment on the said document but to also make a substantial contribution to it in the light of the unfolding new role of Orthodoxy—to remove the bushel and let the light of Orthodoxy shine forth with more clarity and radiance.

I am certain that this gathering is not one of the many that are held from time to time so that the interest in the ecumenical movement might be rekindled. It is high time that we give additional strength to it and help it to rediscover its proper theological direction lest we be caught offering only lip service to it.

I am most heartened by the fact that the WCC (as well as the NCC here in America) is reaching for the theological substantiation and justification of its socioeconomic concerns. I am, as we all are, praying that the seemingly endless theological discussions may open the vistas that we all anticipate and challenge us with the need for some bolder decisions and actions.

I personally believe that only a united Christianity will be able to arrest the cataclysmic forces of negation and self-righteousness that menace with drowning the hopes of the world for a better future. The time runs short unless we can prove even at the last moment that we have the brigades and the legions of spiritual and moral armies to combat the openly unleashed forces of materialism, Marxism and atheism.

We Christians owe it to the martyrs of ancient and contemporary Christianity through whose testimony and martyrdom Christian religion prevailed to prove our own faith and determination to change the course of modern history and rechart the path towards the dominance of the Christian values and ideals.

May God bless this ecumenical assembly gathered by the power of the Holy Spirit!

Response to Archbishop Iakovos' Welcome

METROPOLITAN CHRYSOSTOMOS

MANY THANKS TO YOU, Your Eminence, for your very kind words of welcome to this group of representatives of all the Orthodox and Oriental Church members of the World Council of Churches at this Consultation on BEM, being held in this great Greek Orthodox Theological School of your Archdiocese. Many thanks also to everyone who has had the kindness to greet us on this occasion.

Really, we are very happy for this opportunity to be with all of you, to receive your hospitality, to exchange experiences, and to discuss with the faculty, the bishops, clergy and theologians, who have a direct interest in our subject. This subject is one of the most important for the WCC, for the member Churches, and of course for the whole of Orthodoxy. Our Churches are awaiting from this Consultation fruitful and constructive results, that will provide the needed theological material for a response from the Orthodox Churches to the BEM text, and further clarification on what "reception" means for us Orthodox. We have a big job to accomplish here, during these days.

As you know, the Consultation is to hear a number of specific papers, which will be presented by theologians of the Orthodox and the Oriental Churches, which belong to the same family. Here, let me interject that, through the initiative of the Ecumenical Patriarchate, the dialogue between the Orthodox and Oriental Churches has been reactivated.

After having received and discussed the papers, the Consultation must come to some concrete conclusions and make some specific proposals to our mother Churches, with the view of facilitating their own responsibility for responding officially, by the end of this year, to the Faith and Order Commission, after further and deeper evaluations of the BEM text.

3

Let us hope that the Holy Spirit will lead us to productive deliberations. Towards this aim we ask—Your Eminence and beloved brothers
and sisters—for your prayers and encouragement.

To you, Your Eminence, we want to express our deep gratitude for
having the kindness to come here to greet us. We know that your time
is very precious. We thank you for this, but also for all the manifesta-
tions of love and attention which you have expressed to us through the
hospitality given to our group by Holy Cross Greek Orthodox School
of Theology, through the assistance of yourself and of your collaborators, especially His Grace Bishop Methodios of Boston, the professors and staff of this theological school and all the others who will
help us during our stay and study here.

Once more, Your Eminence, many thanks. Εἰς πολλά ἔτη
Δέσποτα.

A Message to the Rev Dr Emilio Castro, General Secretary of WCC

METROPOLITAN CHRYSOSTOMOS

IT IS A PRIVILEGE and honor for me, as chairman of this Consultation, but also in my capacity as vice-president of the Central Committee of the World Council of Churches, to present to this gathering the Rev Dr Emilio Castro, General Secretary of the Council.

Dr Emilio Castro has had the kindness, being in the States, to come to Boston and greet us, representatives of the Orthodox and the Oriental Churches, in session here in this Greek Orthodox theological school, gathered with the main aim to study the BEM text and to achieve in some deliberations that which will be of great help for our Churches—in view of facilitating them, we hope, in their own responsibility of responding officially to the Faith and Order Commission after further and deeper evaluation of the Lima document itself.

Dr Emilio Castro, the new General Secretary of the World Council of Churches, has many and precious qualifications. Among them I want to underline his remarkable positive disposition in favor of Orthodoxy and of the Orthodox presence and participation in the life and activities of the WCC. I remember his first declaration after his nomination as well as his warm words during his first visit to the Ecumenical Patriarchate last January 6, when he expressed his own desire and determination to see the Orthodox participation in the activities of the World Council of Churches more and more effective and positive. Dr Emilio Castro is definitely a friend of Orthodoxy. We are grateful to him for that.

And with these sentiments we thank him for coming here and being among us today and I ask him to give us kindly the occasion now to hear from him a message of greeting from the WCC.

Seated, left to right: Metropolitan Chrysostomos, Archbishop Iakovos, Metropolitan Emilianos, and Bishop Maximos with participants of the Symposium.

A Message to Participants of the Symposium on BEM

EMILIO CASTRO

Your Eminence Metropolitan Chrysostomos,
Your Graces,
Honored Professors,
Beloved Brothers and Sisters in Christ:

GREETINGS TO YOU from the World Council of Churches, represented here by the Commission on Faith and Order for this symposium on the Orthodox Church's reception of the convergence document, *Baptism, Eucharist, and Ministry.* I am especially pleased to bring you my personal greetings and feel great joy at the coincidence of my being in the United States during your Consultation.

I want to underscore the importance of this symposium and of the Orthodox participation in the World Council of Churches. Since I have come to Geneva in this new position, I have often been asked what differences I find between the Church in Latin America and in Geneva. I respond again and again: Orthodoxy. In Orthodox liturgy, in Orthodox spirituality, in Orthodox theology—the rich gifts of Orthodoxy are unmistakable at the World Council. In particular, I treasure the theological perspective you bring. After all, the WCC is not "their" Council, it is "your" Council.

As I was reading through the documents which arrived in Geneva before this Consultation, I noticed that many of you seemed to be responding to BEM in a fashion reminiscent of Symeon: "My eyes have seen salvation!" At long last, you seemed to be saying, we can recognize ourselves in the work of the Council. This is no small step toward the unity at the heart of the Council's work, and it is due largely to the patient work of Faith and Order. The maturity of the BEM document represents many long years of dialogue and serious theological discussion.

But unlike Symeon, you cannot now rest. It is now time to help your Churches respond. This symposium is an important step toward that process of reception on which you are focusing your discussions this week. In one sense this symposium is an internal discussion. The BEM document raises many questions. Someone asked me, for instance, if because I was baptized a Roman Catholic, am I considered to be the first Catholic General Secretary of WCC? I leave that to you theologians and your counterparts in other communions; what does baptism mean in the context of our life together? One way in which those questions become most obvious at the World Council is in the work of the staff in Geneva. We have a good Orthodox representation, but we also hope that you will not turn aside when we ask for service from your sons and daughters.

However, because of BEM, these discussions are also not internal. Two weeks ago I was in Bulgaria and there received the Order of St. Cyril and Methodios. We might look lightly at such things, but in reality I am spiritually Orthodox now! In legal terms, the title implies the right to speak, so I will take that opportunity today! I will ask you to consider two things especially in your official response to BEM.

First, please be Orthodox in your response. As I understand your Church Fathers and your Tradition, yours is a particularly doxological communion. In our Roman Catholic and Protestant discussions, we have too often stressed the juridical and logical matters of theology. You have honored the mystery, the ultimately unexplainable quality of God. We Occidentals may have forgotten too often what you teach us in your liturgy: that theology is the expression of the mind of the people and the people expresses itself doxologically.

Secondly, do remember that the Church is the Body of Christ for the salvation of the world. In baptism and chrismation, when the Spirit is given it is given not solely for the individual but for the world. "Be my witnesses." Let us not lose our mission understanding in new situations, in the diaspora's marginalization. While you often grow weary of our Protestant sense that in the eucharist we may learn "along the way" toward unity by sharing the bread and wine together now, we Protestants also understand that you cannot agree to eucharistic sharing until the unity is visible in full. Let's keep that dialogue open. But let us also remember that our baptism involves us in the mission of Christ, that the eucharist constitutes us as the Church for others, and that the ministry equips the saints for mission in the world.

From left to right: Frs. Gennadios Limouris, Alkiviadis Calivas, Ion Bria, Dr Emilio Castro, Metropolitan Chrysostomos, Dr Günther Gassmann, and Fr. George Tsetsis.

Introduction

GENNADIOS LIMOURIS

THE MEETING WHICH TOOK PLACE from 11—18 June 1985 at Hellenic College/Holy Cross Greek Orthodox School of Theology in Brookline, MA, USA was an historical event of great importance for the ecumenical movement and for the Orthodox Churches, too. More than forty-five hierarchs and theologians[1] from Eastern Orthodox and Oriental Orthodox Churches from all over the world gathered together for an Inter-Orthodox Symposium on "Baptism, Eucharist and Ministry," the so-called Lima document.

The hosts of this historical gathering were the Greek Orthodox Archdiocese of North and South America and Hellenic College/Holy Cross Greek Orthodox School of Theology. It was prepared and organized by the Orthodox Task Force of the World Council of Churches and the Faith and Order Commission which made possible such a widely representative meeting.

The Symposium and its History

It is well known in the ecumenical world that the World Council and its member churches are in the midst of a process of discussing and responding to the significant theological convergence document on "Baptism, Eucharist and Ministry" (BEM), the so-called "reception process." This document was discerned and elaborated by the Faith and Order Commission in collaboration with eminent and expert theologians of different confessions.

After many years of hard work and many human sacrifices, it was adopted by the January 1982 meeting of the Plenary Commission on Faith and Order in Lima, Peru (2—16 January). The Sixth Assembly

---

[1] See list of participants.

11

of the World Council at Vancouver in 1983 recommended the following timetable to the member churches for responding to this great and important ecumenical document:

> By 31 December 1984 the churches should send in a short report on how the process of the official response is pursued; the deadline for the official response is 31 December 1985.[2]

Following discussions on the preparations of responses to BEM at the Orthodox meeting during the Central Committee of the World Council in July 1984, it was suggested and approved that the Orthodox Task Force of the World Council and the Faith and Order Commission will jointly undertake the organization and preparation of such an Inter-Orthodox Symposium. The main goal of the Symposium was to facilitate, help and clarify a number of questions which might arise, in particular to the Orthodox Churches, when they consider their response to the Lima document. Therefore, the theme of the Symposium was "The Reception of BEM from an Orthodox Perspective."

During a year of preparation and close collaboration the Orthodox Task Force and Faith and Order worked together to the successful realization of this inter-Orthodox gathering in friendly relationship with the Dean of the Holy Cross Greek Orthodox School of Theology, Rev Dr A. Calivas.

The Symposium

On 11 June, the Symposium started with Vespers celebrated in the Holy Cross Chapel, presided by His Grace Methodios, Bishop of Boston, and sung by students of Holy Cross School of Theology.

Bishop Methodios and Dean Calivas welcomed the participants who had arrived from all over the world.

On behalf of the participants His Eminence Metropolitan Chrysostomos of Myra, one of the Vice-Moderators of the WCC Central Committee who also chaired the meeting, thanked the host School and the Bishop, and concluded by saying that ". . . may God bless us during these days of important work that has to be done . . . "

The next day, 12 June, the solemn opening session took place in the auditorium of the Maliotis Cultural Center with the presence of the host of the Symposium, Archbishop Iakovos, Primate of the Greek Orthodox Archdiocese of North and South America, and eminent guests and representatives of different denominations in the Boston area, such

---

[2] VI Assembly of the World Council of Churches. Official Report. Vancouver, Canada, 24 July—10 August, 1983, *Gathered for Life,* ed. David Gill, WCC, Geneva, 1983, p. 47.

as Bishop Alfred Hughes (representing Cardinal Law), Rector of St. John's Roman Catholic Seminary; Rev James Nash, Executive Director, Massachusetts Council of Churches; Rev David Carlson (representing Bishop Harold Wimmer), New England Synod, Lutheran Church in America; Dr Lorine Getz, Executive Director, Boston Theological Institute; Bishop Methodios, Greek Orthodox Diocese of Boston; the Rt Rev Job, OCA Bishop of Hartford; Fr Damon Geiger, Rector of St. Gregory's Seminary; Dr Jane Smith, Associate Dean, Harvard Divinity School; Rev Dr Richard J. Clifford, SJ, Dean, Weston School of Theology; Fr Thomas FitzGerald, President of the Orthodox Theological Society of America; Dr David Covel, Jr, Executive Director of the Massachusetts Bible Society; and professors of the Holy Cross Greek Orthodox School of Theology.

Metropolitan Chrysostomos opened the session with doxological Trinitarian invocation and prayer:

> In the name of the Father and of the Son and of the Holy Spirit. It is a privilege and honor for me to declare the opening of this inter-Orthodox Symposium on the Lima text. May the name of our triune God be blessed. This morning's first plenary will be dedicated to the presentation of greetings of several distinguised church personalities who honor our meeting with their presence, and above all His Eminence Archbishop Iakovos to whom we all are grateful for being present at this opening session.

> Before giving the floor to the various speakers, I wish to express, from this chair, our cordial thanks to the Holy Cross Greek Orthodox School of Theology and its faculty and staff for the generous hospitality they are offering to us during these days.

Dean Calivas called on the guests and church representatives to deliver their messages and expectations for this unique occasion and also on the Director of the Secretariat of the Faith and Order Commission, Rev Dr Günther Gassmann, who particularly thanked Archbishop Iakovos for the generous hospitality and the good fellowship at such a great and important meeting; he expressed his hope for concrete results which would be useful not only for the Orthodox Churches, but also for the ecumenical movement. Archbishop Iakovos, as host of this meeting, then gave his message to the participants. The Primate of the Greek Orthodox Archdiocese of North and South America, this great spiritual and pastoral personality, has for more than twenty-five years assumed the Greek Orthodox leadership in America; he is a former president of the World Council and one of "the foremost ecumenists of our time." The lifetime of Archbishop Iakovos spans over the creative years of ecumenical development in the twentieth century. The ecumenical and interreligious achievements of the Archbishop have to be seen against the general background of the time and place in which we live. His work in Orthodox ecumenism, as he used to say, is a study in the *praxis* of ecumenism.[3] Once he affirmed that "the ecumenical problem is for us the problem of the *disunity* of Christendom and the necessity of the recovery of the biblical patristic synthesis of faith which is constitutive of the one Church."[4]

Archbishop Iakovos, through his own thoughts, emphasized the importance of the Symposium:

> I am certain that this gathering is not one of the many that are held from time to time so that the interest in the ecumenical movement might be rekindled. It is high time that we give additional strength to it and help it to rediscover its proper theological direction lest we be caught offering only lip service to it. . . . I personally believe that only a united Christianity will be able to arrest the cataclysmic forces of negation and self-righteousness that menace with drowning the hopes of the world for a better future.[5]

On behalf of the participants, Metropolitan Chrysostomos replied to Archbishop Iakovos and thanked him for the very kind words and the generous hospitality offered by the Greek Orthodox Archdiocese and Holy Cross; he concluded by saying that ". . . Our Churches are awaiting from this Consultation fruitful and constructive results that will provide the needed theological material for a response from the Orthodox Churches to the BEM text, and further clarification on what "reception" means for us Orthodox, . . . "[6] and he closed the official opening session. A reception followed at the Salle of the Center, which offered a good opportunity for an exchange of opinion, talks and discussions with Archbishop Iakovos and an official photograph was taken. This was the first day of this historical event.

On the same afternoon we had the great pleasure of having with us— even if only for a few hours—the General Secretary of the World Council of Churches, Rev Dr Emilio Castro, travelling officially in the States; he participated in a dinner, offered by His Grace Bishop Methodios.

The next morning the General Secretary participated in the plenary

---

[3] Robert Stephanopoulos, *Archbishop Iakovos as Ecumenist,* in *History of the Greek Orthodox Church in America,* ed. Dr. M. B. Efthimiou and George A. Christopoulos, Greek Orthodox Archdiocese of North and South America, New York, 1984, p. 353.

[4] Ibid., p. 362.

[5] See Archbishop Iakovos' message.

[6] See Metropolitan Chrysostomos' response to Archbishop Iakovos' message.

session and was welcomed by Metropolitan Chrysostomos of Myra who thanked him for his kindness for attending and greeting the assembly. The metropolitan described Dr Castro's qualifications and added: "Among them I want to underline his remarkable positive disposition in favor of Orthodoxy and of the Orthodox presence and participation in the life and activities of the WCC . . . "[7] In replying to the chairman's message, Dr Castro expressed his warm thanks "Since I have come to Geneva in this new position, I have often been asked what differences I find between the Church in Latin America and in Geneva. I respond again and again: Orthodoxy. In Orthodox liturgy, in Orthodox spirituality, in Orthodox theology—the rich gifts of Orthodoxy are unmistakable at the World Council. In particular, I treasure the theological perspective you bring. After all, the WCC is not "their" Council, it is "your" Council. . . . I noticed that many of you seemed to be responding to BEM in a fashion reminiscent of Symeon: "My eyes have seen salvation!"[8]

After this warm exchange of words, and in the same spirit of hope for unity of our churches, Metropolitan Chrysostomos offered Dr Castro, on behalf of the Dean and the professors, the Cross of the Holy Cross as a sign of fellowship and recognition and remembrance of his passage at this historical place and meeting. Pictures and an exchange of greetings followed.

In general the Symposium was characterized by a very good spirit of fellowship and collaboration between the participants. The Spirit of God was present among us and guided us during our stay at Holy Cross.

Metropolitan Chrysostomos of Myra had assumed the important task of leadership. With his broad theological education from the University of Rome to the University of Strasbourg, with his long experience not only as Professor of Dogmatics at the Patriarchal School of Theology in Halki/Constantinople, this eminent theologian has been well-known in the ecumenical movement for more than thirty years; at present he is Vice-Moderator of the WCC Central Committee and a former member of the Faith annd Order Commission and a member of the Holy Synod of the Ecumenical Patriarchate. He is also author of various articles. His presence at our gathering left a real mark.

In this difficult task of leadership he was ably assisted by the Moderator of the Orthodox Task Force, Rev Prof Ion Bria; the Representative of the Ecumenical Patriarchate in the World Council, the V Rev G. Tsetsis; and the Faith and Order Secretariat, Rev Dr G. Gassmann and Rev Dr G. Limouris.

---

[7] See message of Metropolitan Chrysostomos of Myra to the Rev Dr Emilio Castro.

[8] See response by Rev Dr Emilio Castro.

The plenary sessions were also moderated by a number of participants, and the drafting committee was under the responsibility of not only an old friend of the Faith and Order Commission, but my professor, Prof N. Lossky from the Orthodox Institute of St. Sergius, Paris, France.

The Report

"It appears to us that we, as Orthodox, should welcome the Lima document as an experience of a new stage in the history of the ecumenical movement. After centuries of estrangements, hostility and mutual ignorance, divided Christians are seeking to speak together on essential aspects of ecclesial life, namely baptism, eucharist and ministry. This process is unique in terms of the wide attention which the Lima document is receiving in all the churches. We rejoice in the fact that Orthodox theologians have played a significant part in the formulation of this document."[9]

This paragraph comes from the report which was elaborated by the participants and shows the results of this important gathering. Therefore the participants express appreciation for the Lima document and they see in it "a remarkable ecumenical document of doctrinal convergence. It is, therefore, to be highly commended for its serious attempt to bring to light and express today 'the faith of the Church throughout the ages.' "[10] "In many sections, this faith of the Church is clearly expressed . . . " They ask the Orthodox Churches "to facilitate the use of the BEM document for study and discussion on different levels of the Church's life" and to be "open to reading BEM and to responding to it in a spirit of critical self-examination . . . "

The report also lists a number of examples of "issues which we believe need further clarification and elaboration" or which are not addressed in BEM. Among such examples are the relationship between the unity of the Church and baptismal unity, the relationship of the eucharist to ecclesiology, the distinction between the priesthood of the entire people of God and the ordained priesthood. The report concludes with suggestions and perspectives for future Faith and Order work.

Papers were presented by Metropolitan Chrysostomos of Myra (Ecumenical Patriarchate); Metropolitan Anthony of Transylvania (Romanian Orthodox Church); Archbishop Kirill of Smolensk (Russian Orthodox Church); Bishop Nerses Bozabalian (Armenian Apostolic Church); and by Rev Professors K. M. George (Orthodox Syrian Church of the East), Thomas Hopko (Orthodox Church in America),

---

[9] See Report of the Inter-Orthodox Symposium.

[10] Preface to BEM, p. x.

Nikos Nissiotis (University of Athens), and Theodore Stylianopoulos (Holy Cross Greek Orthodox School of Theology); Rev Dr G. Gassmann and Rev Dr G. Limouris from the Faith and Order Secretariat presented introductory papers.

Conclusion of the Meeting

In the course of the Symposium the participants were hosted at dinners sponsored by His Grace Bishop Methodios of Boston, by the Council of Eastern Orthodox Churches of Central Massachusetts, and by the Pan-Orthodox Clergy Fellowship of Boston.

After a week of fruitful and successful deliberations the Symposium ended its work on 17 June. On behalf of all participants, Metropolitan Chrysostomos expressed thanks to the Dean, professors and collaborators of the Holy Cross Greek Orthodox School of Theology for their moral and material support:

I would like to take this opportunity to extend my sincere gratitude and thanks to a number of individuals and groups who have extended us hospitality and provided services to this Inter-Orthodox Symposium:

—to the Holy Cross Greek Orthodox School of Theology, especially to the President, Dr Thomas C. Lelon; the Dean, Fr Alkiviadis Calivas; to the professors and their collaborators for their significant contributions to our comfortable stay as well as to our reflections on this most important issue facing all the churches today;

—to the Orthodox Task Force of the World Council of Churches and its former Moderator, Fr George Tsetsis, and the actual Moderator, Fr Ion Bria, and the other members of the group in Geneva for their continual attention to the concerns of Orthodoxy in the life and work of the Council;

—to the Faith and Order Commission, under the leadership of Rev Dr Günther Gassmann, and to staff members, especially Rev Dr Gennadios Limouris, for their historical perspectives on the work of the Commission and the development of the BEM text and for their guidance in our work here this week;

—to His Grace, Bishop Methodios of Boston, for his spiritual support of the work of all the Orthodox Churches gathered together in this place;

—to the chairmen and the secretaries of the groups for their very inspired work, and to the drafting committee, which under the intelligent and creative leadership of Professor Lossky, gave us one of the best report papers;

—to Mrs Artemis Gyftopoulos, Director of the Maliotis Cultural

Center, and to William Gushes, without whose assistance this Symposium would not have proceeded as smoothly as it has;
—to Carol Thysell of the National Council Faith and Order staff, for her secretarial assistance;
—and to the students and stewards of Hellenic College and Holy Cross Greek Orthodox School of Theology who have attempted to make our stay pleasant.

As we leave this place, let us pray that the Holy Spirit will guide us in our diakonia in our Churches.''

A Doxology took place in the Chapel, where the Dean of Holy Cross, accompanied by the professors, offered His Eminence Metropolitan Chrysostomos the Great Cross of the School as a *martyria* for his leadership and as a sign of recognition from the School of Theology to this eminent figure of the Great Church of Constantinople. Rev Prof I. Bria and Rev Dr G. Gassmann were also favored with awards.

The New York Event
The generous hospitality of Archbishop Iakovos extended even to New York where on 20 June a representative group of participants, personally invited by the Primate, were received at the Greek Orthodox Archdiocese. A program was prepared and organized by the Greek Orthodox Archdiocese which was in the hands of Presbytera Niki Stephanopoulos, Director of the Office of News and Information of the Archdiocese.

At 15:00 hours a press conference took place with representatives from the written press, TV and radio broadcast, in New York City. Archbishop Iakovos opened the press conference and introduced the Orthodox participants and explained the purpose of the Boston meeting. The journalists raised questions concerning the ecumenical significance of the BEM document; Metropolitan Chrysostomos and Metropolitan Anthony replied on behalf of the group to the various questions, especially the importance of the "reception of the BEM document" in the Orthodox Church and the involvement of the Orthodox Church in the ecumenical movement in general.

Rev Dr G. Gassmann concluded, expressing gratitude to Archbishop Iakovos for the ecumenical event of Boston. A very friendly reception followed in the Salle of feast of the Archdiocese. Many friends of Archbishop Iakovos, church leaders of different denominations were present such as: Metropolitan Theodosius of the Orthodox Church in America; the Armenian Bishop of New York; Dr Arie Brouwer, General Secretary of the National Council of Churches; Brother Jeffrey Gros of the NCCC/Faith and Order Department in New York; Dr William Rusch, Lutheran Church in America; Metropolitan Silas of New Jersey; His Grace Anthimos of Denver; His Grace Philotheos; Bishop Methodios of Boston; V Rev George J. Bacopoulos, Chancellor; Rev Dr N. Michael Vaporis, Dean of Hellenic College.

Metropolitan Chrysostomos thanked Archbishop Iakovos for this friendly atmosphere and genorous hospitality offered by the Primate and wished him to have many more years in his diakonia and concluded: "We have to look forward to the future under the guidance of the Holy Spirit for the profit of our Churches."

The Archbishop presented the guests and offered presents to all participants. On behalf of the Faith and Order Commission, the Director, Rev Dr Günther Gassmann, offered a Genevese engraving to the Archbishop as a sign of gratitude for his pastoral interest in this ecumenical and historical event.

Conclusion

It is our task and obligation to express our deep gratitude and respects to the Greek Orthodox Archdiocese of North and South America and its Primate, Archbishop Iakovos for hosting the Symposium. May God bless him and give him many years "Εἰς πολλὰ ἔτι Δεόποτα" for his diakonia in the United States. Many thanks from our hearts for the friendly hospitality of Hellenic College/Holy Cross Greek Orthodox School of Theology; its President, Dr Thomas Lelon; and its Rector, Rev Dr Alkiviadis Calivas, who untiringly cared for us together with co-workers, particularly Fr Ilia Katre, Mrs Ketches, Fr Thomas FitzGerald, and Savas Zembillas, for their excellent contribution, always in a spirit of fellowship and friendship.

Our thanks go also to the director of the Maliotis Cultural Center, who hosted the Symposium, Mrs Artemis Gyftopoulos and her assistant William Gushes who served us for the best.

We also wish to thank the Director of the Faith and Order Office of the National Council of Churches, Brother Jeffrey Gros, for kindly making available Ms Carol Thysell for secretarial assistance and we appreciate her hard work.

Last, but not least, we express our gratitude to Bishop Methodios of Boston and his assistants for their kindness to host the participants. Finally, the Dean of Hellenic College and editor of *The Greek Orthodox Theological Review,* Rev Dr N. Michael Vaporis, who kindly agreed to publish the acts of the Symposium in the *Review.*

Further thanks are due to the professors and students of Holy Cross as well as to all those who have sent greetings: Rt Rev John B. Coburn, Bishop of the Episcopal Diocese of Massachusetts; Most Rev Joseph

Tawil, Archbishop of the Melkite Diocese of Newton; Rev Alfred E. Williams, Minister and President of the Massachusetts Conference of the United Church of Christ; and Dr Robert Kittrell, Executive Director of the National Conference of Christians and Jews.

The deliberations at the Symposium, under the wise and highly encouraging leadership of Metropolitan Chrysostomos of Myra, have lead to very important insights and results. We express our deep gratitude and respectful recognition; *multos annos* for serving the Orthodox Church and his involvement in the ecumenical movement.

We would also like to say a word of thanks to the two administrative assistants in the Faith and Order Secretariat in Geneva, Mrs Eileen Chapman and Mrs Renate Sbeghen, for their continued assistance in preparing and organizing this meeting.

Rev Dr Günther Gassmann and Rev Dr Gennadios Limouris also visited Boston and Harvard Universities as well as St. Vladimir's Theological Seminary in New York, and had many contacts with professors and fellows of the Boston and New York areas.

We give thanks to God that his Spirit guided us for the love of his Son.

General Introduction

GÜNTHER GASSMANN

THE MOVEMENT (LATER THE COMMISSION) on Faith and Order had from its early stages the benefit of an active Orthodox participation. Already in 1919 all the major Orthodox Churches responded favorably to the invitation to prepare for a World Conference on Faith and Order. At the Faith and Order preparatory conference which took place at Geneva in 1920, several Orthodox Church leaders and theologians participated and used this opportunity to present and interpret the Encyclical Letter of the Ecumenical Patriarchate of 1920, one of the basic and most influential documents of the ecumenical movement. During this early period Orthodox representatives like Archbishop Germanos of Thyateira and Professor Alivizatos played a leading role in Faith and Order.

After the foundation of the World Council of Churches in 1948, Faith and Order became a Commission and after 1961 full Orthodox participation was again possible. I see a remarkable development in this participation. At first there was a certain reluctance on the side of the Orthodox to engage in doctrinal discussions in contrast to an openness for collaboration on social issues since these did not involve doctrinal aspects. The ecumenical discussions in the sixties and seventies, however, made all of us conscious of the fact that the social-ethical issues were also related to doctrinal presuppositions and, as a consequence, created deep tensions within the ecumenical community. Along with this there was the impression that the social-political concerns became a priority for the WCC over against its basic calling to serve the unity of the Church. This development may have contributed to an increasingly active interest and full participation by the Orthodox Churches in the work of the Faith and Order Commission. One sign of this involvement has been the fact that the last two Moderators of

21

the Faith and Order Commission came from Orthodox Churches: Professor Meyendorff (1969-1970) and Professor Nissiotis (1975-1983).

We in Faith and Order are grateful that within the WCC the Orthodox Churches are now among the most committed supporters of our work. We need this support in order to fulfill our fundamental task to call the churches to the visible unity which is given in Jesus Christ and which is an image of the unity of the Holy Trinity. We need this support and active participation also because without the contribution of the rich theological and spiritual treasure of the Orthodox tradition our theological perspectives would be limited to the Western tradition and its divided confessional expressions. Here, the insights and experiences of the Orthodox tradition can help us to look beyond our separate confessions in order to rediscover the fulness of the apostolic faith as it is witnessed in holy Scripture and further developed in the first centuries of Christ's Church in the East and the West.

The Orthodox participation in Faith and Order and the official representation of Roman Catholic theologians in the commission since 1968 have made this commission the most representative theological forum in this world. Yes, it is a theological *forum,* which does not have authority of its own. Accordingly the results of its work will have an impact on the thinking and ecumenical position of the churches only if these results are of a high theological quality and can be accepted by the churches as adequate expositions of the faith of the Church throughout the centuries. The Faith and Order Commission has been created by the churches; its members are appointed on the proposal or with the agreement of the churches; its work is done for the churches and the results of its work are submitted to the churches for their judgment. It is, therefore, not a commission which exists apart from the churches in its own right. It is a commission which belongs to the churches; it is *our* commission.

One of these results of the work of the Faith and Order Commission is, of course, the Lima document on *Baptism, Eucharist and Ministry.* In the short history of Faith and Order this was a most significant achievement after many years of theological dialogue. We cannot know yet how deep the impact of this document will be on the churches. But we notice already that BEM has become the most widely distributed and discussed ecumenical document in the history of the ecumenical movement. More than 300,000 copies in over twenty-five languages have been published and thousands of congregations, ecumenical groups, theological seminaries, theological and ecumenical commissions, etc. are studying this document. This is indeed a unique ecumenical event. So far twenty churches have sent their official response to the

WCC. They generally regard BEM as a most important step forward in our common ecumenical endeavor, but there are also critical questions concerning specific points in BEM. Such critical remarks are often used to make proposals for the future work of Faith and Order. Most of these responses emphasize that the reception process of BEM must also continue after the respective churches have formulated their responses.

I know that it is irritating to many Orthodox when we speak of a BEM 'reception-process.' To clarify this point will be a major task of this symposium, because misunderstandings can easily arise in this connection. It is not my intention to prejudge this clarification, but I would like to indicate that we in Faith and Order are using the expression 'reception process' not in a specific historical or traditional sense. Rather we would like with this expression to refer to the expectation that the churches are receiving this document in order to evaluate it on all levels. It is their task to judge how far this document reflects the faith of the Church through the centuries and where further theological dialogue is necessary. The churches should study this document also with the question in mind as to whether it contains theological perspectives which could enrich their theological thinking and spiritual life and which could help them to come to closer relations with other Christian traditions.

For us non-Orthodox, the contributions of the Orthodox tradition to the elaboration and text of "Baptism, Eucharist and Ministry" are clearly discernible. Many have already welcomed the way in which Orthodox theological and spiritual insights in BEM have the potential to deepen our Western thinking on the sacraments and the ministry. But BEM is of course not an Orthodox document written by Orthodox for the Orthodox. It is, therefore, a task for the Orthodox Churches to consider how far they can recognize the faith of the Church also in those parts of BEM which are not formulated in a traditional Orthodox terminology. This applies, of course, in an analogous way, to all the churches. It belongs to the special character of an ecumenical document that it does not simply reflect the thinking and language of one particular Christian tradition. Such a text is the result of an ecumenical dialogue which seeks to express the common faith. And the interpretation of such a text has to take this into account. Yet, I would like to stress once again the strong Orthodox impact on BEM which might be noticed by us non-Orthodox much more directly than by you yourselves.

In the ecumenical community there is quite widespread curiosity and expectation concerning the Orthodox responses to BEM. How will the Orthodox react? How will they evaluate this endeavor to lead the churches closer to each other in their understanding and practice of baptism, eucharist and ministry? What are the main points of Orthodox critique? There is no doubt that the responses of the Orthodox Churches will be studied with special interest. This will certainly be the case with us in Faith and Order also. We consider the Orthodox responses of the highest importance for the present ecumenical situation as well as for the further work of Faith and Order. Therefore we are happy to be of help in arranging this symposium which, through your efforts and with the guidance of the Holy Spirit, will hopefully render an important contribution to the elaboration of Orthodox responses to BEM.

This is not the first time that representatives of the worldwide Orthodox Church come together in order to exchange their views on an important issue of common concern. The wish to arrange for such a symposium was expressed by Orthodox members of the Central Committee of the WCC. This desire was taken up by the Orthodox Task Force in the WCC which turned to us in Faith and Order for assistance in the preparation of the symposium.

Now you have arrived from all parts of the world, venerable and esteemed representatives of the Orthodox Churches. We are especially happy that both Eastern and Oriental Orthodox Churches are coming together at this symposium. The task of Faith and Order in helping to prepare this meeting is finished—it is now fully your meeting. But our interest in this meeting is not finished, and we are grateful that, together with the three guests from the American churches, we can be present at your deliberations. We are now observers, but our hearts and minds are with you, and we pray that God the Father, the Son and the Holy Spirit will inspire you and will grant his manifold blessings to all of us.

The Physiognomy of BEM after Lima in the Present Ecumenical Situation

GENNADIOS LIMOURIS

WE ARE LIVING IN A CENTURY—the twentieth—which can be described not only as the century of ecclesiology, but also among other things as the century of the ecumenical movement.[1] As the twentieth century dawned, it seemed that a number of signs were present indicating that the isolation and the sectarianism of the churches were coming to an end.[2] Still, few were those who at the beginning of this century would have guessed the ecumenical advances to be made in the next eighty years. The slow and uneven progress since the divisions of the Church was to accelerate sharply. The early part of the twentieth century has often been described as the moment of birth of the ecumenical movement. Different churches have learned—indeed had to learn—that their painful state of separation could no longer be tolerated as a natural condition, and they have been making efforts to put an end to this evil in the Church.

These efforts towards church unity have constantly grown and diversified in an impressive way during the past decades. Contrary to what many may say and assume, we are in the midst of a resurgence of concern for church unity; in that *aggiornamento* the World Council of Churches is playing a crucial role.[3]

---

[1] Cf. O. Dibelius, *Das Jahrhundert der Kirche* (Berlin, 1927); see also J. R. Nelson and K. D. Schmidt in T. Rendtorff, *Kirche und Theologie* (Gütersloh, 1966), p. 11: "Die Kirche bildet eines der Hauptanliegen der Theologie des 20. Jahrhunderts"; J. Karmiris, *Orthodox Ecclesiology* (Athens, 1973), 5, p. 7 (in Greek).

[2] W. G. Rusch, *Ecumenism: A Movement Toward Church Unity* (Philadelphia, 1985), p. 26.

[3] G. Limouris, *The Church as Mystery and Prophetic Sign,* FO/85:8, January 1985, p. 1.

The churches are more or less familiar with this development of unity discussions in the ecumenical era. After the stage of what is called "comparative ecclesiology" in which the positions of the confessional families were carefully set out and compared, differences registered and similarities recognized, a second stage followed which lasted for about a decade during which the churches became more dynamic in terms of mission and event. This new phase is marked by an emphasis on the renewal and reform of the churches. This includes the belief that we understand the Church, not by concentrating on a thing in itself, but by looking beyond the Church to the world for which it exists to serve and to recreate.

From the beginning of the ecumenical movement, Faith and Order had envisaged working for the unity in Christ and considered it a necessary presupposition to contribute to the need of a common witness, "martyria," of Christians and Christian churches. Thus, the Faith and Order Movement focused its attention on the doctrinal issues of disorder and unity.

Leaving behind the hostilities of the past, the churches have now begun to discover many promising convergences in the ecumenical movement in shared convictions and perspectives. These convergences assure us that, despite much diversity in theological expression, the churches have much in common in their understanding of the faith. The resultant document on "Baptism, Eucharist and Ministry" aims at becoming part of a faithful reflection of the common Christian Tradition on essential elements of Christian communion. Therefore, it so happens that, in the providence of God, our churches, and in particular the member churches of the World Council of Churches, are being invited to consider the Lima document, presenting a significant theological convergence which the Commission on Faith and Order was able to discern and to formulate.

For the first time in the history of the ecumenical movement, Faith and Order and the World Council of Churches—with and for its member churches—have offered them a document and process in which—thanks to a new way of looking at the Tradition—all the results of the dialogue between the "old churches" and the "churches of the Reformation," as well as of the dialogues internal to each of these two blocks, have been integrated.

The Ecumenical Roots of Baptism, Eucharist and Ministry (BEM)

To review the whole history of the BEM document—half a century of ecumenical work—in a few lines is no easy task to undertake today. Let us try to underline the most important steps of the earlier history of this "ecumenical process"; it is essential to know about it at least in outline in order to grasp the significance of the Lima decision and the unique character of its statements.

From Lausanne (1927) to Montreal (1963)

By and large, the year 1920 can be regarded as the most important and decisive date of the "incarnation" of the temporary ecumenical movement.

Therefore, at the same time, the preliminary meeting for the World Conference on Faith and Order took place in Geneva and the Orthodox Churches had been invited to participate; nearly all of them had sent delegates,[4] totalling seventeen. These seventeen delegates met in private before the general meeting and decided to follow a common line; Orthodoxy was to be present as a common voice. The Metropolitan of Seleukia, Mgr. Germanos, a representative of the Ecumenical Patriarchate, acted as their spokesman.

Moreover, just before the preliminary meeting on Faith and Order, Metropolitan Germanos, accompanied by two other Orthodox delegates,[5] paid a brief visit to the preliminary meeting on "Life and Work" which was also being held in Geneva. Archbishop Nathan Söderblom from Uppsala[6] also played a crucial role and gave initial impetus to the movement; he had invited them in order to show the "Life and Work" delegates that the Ecumenical Patriarchate was ready to cooperate with the other churches; from the hands of Metropolitan Germanos he received a very important document from the Orthodox Church—the encyclical of the Ecumenical Patriarchate of Constantinople (1920) addressed "Unto the Churches of Christ Everywhere,"[7] indicating the position of the Ecumenical Patriarchate on the restoration of unity between all churches and Christians: "Our own Church holds that rapprochement between the various Christian churches and fellowship between them is not excluded by the doctrinal differences which exist between them. In our opinion such a rapprochement is highly desirable and necessary. It would be useful in many ways for the real interest of each particular church and the whole Christian body,

---

[4] The Russian Orthodox Church could not be represented, but church leaders from the Russian emigration were present.

[5] The two other members of the Orthodox delegation were: Metropolitan of Nubia Nikolaos and Archimandrite Dr. Chrysostomos Papadopoulos (later Archbishop of Athens, 1923-41).

[6] B. Sundkler, *Nathan Söderblom: His Life and Work* (Lund, 1986), pp. 379-80.

[7] The Encyclical had been prepared between 10 January and 19 November 1919 by the Holy Synod of the Ecumenical Patriarchate and it was sent out in January 1920. See the text (translated from Greek) in *The Ecumenical Review*, 12 (1959) 79.

and also for the preparation and advancement of that blessed union which will be completed in the future in accordance with the will of God . . . so that they (churches) should no more consider one another as strangers and foreigners, but as relatives, and as being a part of the household of God and 'fellow heirs, members of the same body and partakers of the promise of God in Christ (Eph 3.6)' ''.[8]

Metropolitan Chrysostomos of Myra raises the question as to why the Ecumenical Patriarchate tried to take the initiative. In his opinion the answer is the following: "Because it was once again—but more urgently and more definitely than in the past—asked to define its position against the separated Christian churches. And this position was dictated by its divine origin as a Church, by its pneumatocentric teaching, by its experience in the relations with other churches and confessions, and finally by its conscience of being an institution which should undertake pioneer work in order to define its position vis-a-vis the horrible and unacceptable fact of division."[9]

After the formation of the League of Nations, the Ecumenical Patriarchate of Constantinople envisaged the possibility that churches could establish a similar league. This was the first initiative in the genesis of the WCC as it exists today. Therefore, this encyclical was also the first official proposal from any church for the founding—in spite of dogmatic difficulties—of a Council of Churches at a world level with a specific program in order to encourage the gradual realization of the ecclesial *communio*. This initiative "without precedence in the history of the Church"[10] greatly encouraged Archbishop Söderblom in his endeavors. For the Ecumenical Patriarchate in general this document provided the basis for sustained cooperation by all churches with the very important ecclesiological consequence that in spite of the ecclesiological self-understanding of the Orthodox Churches it was addressed to "all churches of Christ." The natural result was that the Orthodox shared in the founding of the World Council of Churches in Amsterdam in 1948 thus preventing it from being a "pan-Protestant" movement and enabling it to be a meeting place for all Christian traditions despite the complete absence of the Roman Catholic Church at that time.[11]

---

[8] Ibid.

[9] Metropolitan of Myra Chrysostomos (Konstantinidis), *La position de l'Orthodoxie dans le monde chrétien actuel* (conference given in Athens on 20 February, 1985), see *Episkepsis* no. 331 (January, 3, 1985), p. 18 (in French).

[10] W. A. Visser't Hooft, *The Genesis and Formation of the World Council of Churches* (Geneva, 1982), p. 1.

[11] A. Papaderos, " 'Die Pferdebremse' vor Gericht. Zum Streit um das 'politische' Engagement des ÖRK," in *Ökumenische Rundschau,* 30 (1984) 409.

Throughout the history of the World Council of Churches the Orthodox Church never lost sight of this principle, particularly since the trinitarian addition to the WCC basis which was theologically so important for the Orthodox and which was revised at the New Delhi Assembly in 1961 in accordance with the wishes and conceptions of the Orthodox Church. Since then all the Orthodox Churches have actively participated in the work of the World Council of Churches; hence the World Council is not anything alien to Orthodoxy, but can be seen as its own organization (as can be seen in the encyclical of the Ecumenical Patriarchate at the occasion of the twenty-fifth anniversary of the World Council or the message from the Moscow Patriarchate) and has been a voice from within the Council, deeply committed to the continuation of its work without losing sight of its real aim: to achieve full communion of the churches on the basis of true belief and love.

I have mentioned all these events in the 1920s because I am convinced that these dates marked a very important step, beginning with the initiative of the Orthodox Church towards an ecumenism which was to find its achievement later in the genesis of the Lima document.

It is now more than fifty years since in Lausanne, in 1927, when the first steps were taken towards discussing a subject which should be of interest to the whole of Christianity. After centuries of separation and dire estrangement, the attempt was now to be made to mend the torn robe of Jesus Christ in order that the divided members of his mystical Body, the Church, might again be bound together. Therefore, at this First World Conference, Faith and Order was entrusted with the question of sacramental unity (Baptism and Eucharist) and also the questions relating to the ministries of the Church. However, the results achieved in Lausanne fell far short of the high-flown expectations.

From the present vantage point, the surprising factor is not that agreement proved impossible right away at this first ecumenical conference, but rather that people had the courage at that time to tackle at one and the same time this and other central ecumenical questions which still preoccupy us today. After Lausanne, there was hardly any major Commission meeting at which these three issues did not play a significant role and were further illuminated by ecumenical experiences.

At the Third World Conference on Faith and Order, in Lund in 1952, it was realized that no progress towards unity would be achieved by a comparative method alone. The Conference looked for progress in two directions. It affirmed the need for the churches to act together in those matters where deep differences of conviction did not compel them to act separately (i.e. ecumenism is not simply concerned with doctrine, but also with living, worshipping and acting). It also recommended that in the future the doctrine of the Church should be studied "in close relation both to the doctrine of Christ and to the doctrine of the Holy Spirit." The full trinitarian thrust became clear at the Fourth World Conference on Faith and Order held at Montreal in 1963. In the doctrine of the Holy Trinity the Church expresses its faith that unity in diversity is at the heart of God himself.

Faith and Order began to spend less time comparing the "branches of the tree" and more time exploring the "common trunk" and the roots—exploring what Scripture and Tradition have said about ministry, sacraments and the nature of the Church. The old dichotomy between Scripture and Tradition was left behind:

> By the *Tradition* is meant the Gospel itself, transmitted from generation to generation in and by the Church, Christ himself present in the life of the Church. By *tradition* is meant the traditionary process.[12]

From Bristol (1967) to Lima (1982)

In 1965, the Faith and Order Commission began to elaborate the theme of the Holy Eucharist, and two years later, in 1967, a first draft document was presented to the Bristol Commission. In Bristol it was proposed that the earlier study on the Eucharist be enlarged to include concerns of baptism and confirmation as well, and, in 1971, concerns of the "ordained ministry" were added. The whole "pre-process" work found its interim form in the three agreed statements "One Baptism, One Eucharist and a Mutually Recognized Ministry" (Accra, 1974).

In 1975, the Fifth Assembly of the World Council of Churches in Nairobi expressed its appreciation of these convergence statements and recommended that the Accra document be sent to all member churches for study and comment. This first round of "reception" of the Accra texts took place during the years 1976 and 1978. The response was overwhelming: more than one hundred responses reached the Secretariat on Faith and Order from all parts of the world. Therefore, a small theological steering committee, under the leadership of Frere Max Thurian, was established—with a very important and significant Orthodox participation. The results of four years' work of this committee constituted the basis of the concluding discussion at the Lima Commission meeting in 1982.

---

[12]P. C. Rodger/L. Vischer (eds.), *The Fourth World Conference on Faith and Order, Montreal 1963,* New York Association Press, 1964, "Section 2 Report," p. 50.

Lima (1982) and After

This ecumenical document—the result of more than half a century of study and dialogue—found its culmination in Lima (Peru) when over 100 theologians from all over the world met and unanimously approved the "maturity" of "Baptism, Eucharist and Ministry" proceeding from the Accra Commission meeting (1974). Theologians from all major church traditions were represented in Lima—Roman Catholic, Anglican, Orthodox, Baptist, Lutheran, Methodist, Reformed, and others.

In the course of the Lima meeting 190 proposed alterations of the text were considered. On 12 January, the following motion was put before the Commission: "The Commission considers the revised text on *Baptism, Eucharist and Ministry* to have been brought to such a stage of maturity that it is now ready for transmission to the churches in accordance with the mandate given at the Fifth Assembly of the World Council of Churches in Nairobi, 1975, and reaffirmed by the Central Committee in Dresden, 1981."[13]

The vote was taken on the document as a whole, not on each section. The motion passed unanimously, without negative votes or abstentions.

The Vancouver Assembly of the World Council of Churches (1983) emphasized the importance of the spiritual process of the BEM reception and encouraged the churches to submit their official response by 31 December 1985. The World Council has already received twenty-one official responses, among them the response from the Russian Orthodox Church.

Ecumenical Significance

We live today at a crucial moment in the history of humankind. As churches grow in unity, they are also asking themselves how their understanding and practice of Baptism, Eucharist and Ministry relate to their mission in and for the renewal of the human community as they seek to promote justice, peace and reconciliation. Therefore, our understanding of BEM cannot be divorced from the redemptive and liberating mission of Christ through the churches in the modern world.

It also needs to be said that the World Council does not expect each Church to adopt the language of the text as *official dogma;* and yet, something much more significant than another round of theological exchange is now called for and expected. The theologians have said in effect: "There is no good reason why we cannot put the historic

---

[13]M. Kinnamon (ed.), *Towards Visible Unity. Commission on Faith and Order, Lima 1982,* vol. 1, Faith and Order Paper No. 112, (Geneva, 1982), pp. 83-84.

disputes over the sacraments and ministry behind us"—they have reached a "convergence." The reception process will obviously be far from easy!

Therefore, BEM is not an isolated event—nor was it produced only for the pleasure and "profit" of theologians. It is one of the essential marks of unity as conciliar fellowship which the Nairobi Assembly in 1975 identified as the goal of the ecumenical movement.

Speaking as a convergence statement, the Lima document is more humble, more anticipatory. BEM is not a negative judgment—only a realistic one. It reminds the churches of the fact that the ecumenical pilgrimage has not yet reached its goal and that the measure of unity, which can be expressed now, by far exceeds the timidity of our dialogues and conferences. Quite rightly, this document is not described as a consensus document or a consensus statement, but as a document containing statements on convergence since consensus in the sense of the word was not reached on the themes discussed—as has been pointed out several times in the document. In the nature of things, this creates additional difficulties with regard to its reception and the type of reception aimed at. Hence, one comment made in the preface is misleading, i.e. "that theologians of such widely differing traditions should have been able to speak so harmoniously about baptism, eucharist and ministry is unprecedented in the modern ecumenical movement."[14] This sounds as if the document were adopted in its present form. It is, of course, a wonderful thing that the document was adopted in its present form. That theologians from different traditions also traditionally holding differing views were able to concur in one and the same document and to reach a certain degree of harmony or even conformity, is a sign of qualification. This is already a great step forward. Lukas Vischer used a somewhat more cautious wording in the preface to the Accra document: "It cannot be taken as a matter of course that theologians of widely differing traditions should be able to speak with one voice in so many respects on baptism, eucharist and ministry."[15] The debt of the Lima document to the text just mentioned is obvious.

While the core, or nucleus, of this text reflects the ecumenical work up to the present day, it also illustrates a new way of approaching the centuries-old debate on these three issues among the Christian confessions. And this convergence document, as a result of genuine ecumenical dialogue within the fellowship of Christian churches and in mutual appreciation of one another's tradition and charismatic

---

[14]BEM, Preface, 9.

[15]G. Müller-Fahrenholz (Hg), *Eine Taufe, eine Eucharistie, ein Amt* (Frankfurt/Main, 1976), p. 3.

life, presents the converging lines of the faith of the separated churches on baptism, eucharist and ministry.

Only this can explain the reason the separated church confessions—from the extreme Catholic to the extreme Protestant—can now together, and in full agreement, state items of faith on BEM which seemed impossible even a few years ago. This is the "new understanding" of "consensus" in a positive sense, i.e. confirming in common our basic elements of faith.

The document is also of special significance because of the methodology that was used to bring it about. Until the 1950s, Faith and Order frequently was a place where Protestant churches compared their conceptions of doctrinal questions (Augsburg vs Westminster vs Thirty-Nine Articles), but after Lund (1952) the work took a decisive turn. Faith and Order began to explore what Scripture and church Tradition had to say. The tradition of the Gospel, the *paradosis* of the *kerygma,* the faith of the Apostolic Church, testified in the Scripture and transmitted as a living reality through the ages, is what the churches have asked their theologians in Faith and Order to explore and express—and this, they now claim to have done with regard to "Baptism, Eucharist, and Ministry."

However, though it is a major event in the process towards visible unity—and for this reason one understands why it has been welcomed in ecumenical circles and by the international press with such enthusiasm—we must nevertheless guard ourselves against any kind of triumphalism and self-justification.

Consultations on BEM

One of the ecumenical bodies dealing with BEM is the Conference of European Churches (CEC). The European churches, and in particular the CEC, bear a major responsibility for the development of the Christian Tradition over the centuries, and also for the divisions which have separated Christians into different confessions or communions. Therefore, the CEC—in close cooperation with the Faith and Order Commission—has drawn up a program of four regional consultations looking particularly at the European discussion of BEM and its "reception." The aim of the CEC in this was not to substitute itself for its member churches with a view to providing a global response to BEM in their place, but to take the opportunity of examining certain factors that may contribute to the reception of BEM by the European churches—since the two main directions of the work of the CEC are service to peace and service to ecumenism in Europe.

The first consultation held at Bucharest (Rumania), 25-27 June 1984, focused upon "The influence of European philosophy and ways of thought (Geistesgeschichte) on the reception of BEM in the different church traditions." It pointed out that some Christian divisions in Europe had in fact been the result of a false dualism between matter and spirit. As a result of this dualism there had been a tendency to polarization between those who were affected by rationalism (for example, regarding the eucharist as a mere memorial of a past event), and those who were affected by excessive realism (for example, regarding the eucharistic elements as not losing their former mode of existence as bread and wine). BEM had overcome this dualism by a properly biblical understanding of the relationship of spirit and matter, whereby the Holy Spirit in Christ sanctified the human being as a whole.

European culture had also been excessively influenced by individualization and privatization. BEM restored a proper degree of catholicity and the universal impact of baptism, eucharist and ministry.

The second consultation held at Iserlohn (FRG), 10-14 December 1984, had as its theme "The influence of confessional and church self-understanding on the reception of BEM and the consequences of such reception." The papers presented and the reports of the three sections of the consultation showed that confessional self-understanding can exert influence on the reception of BEM in two different ways:

(a) If confessional self-understanding remains enclosed in itself and fails to take into account the apostolic faith in all its fullness, then the BEM reception process will be transformed into a process which merely hardens their previous confessional attitudes.

(b) But if confessional self-understanding remains open to the whole of the apostolic faith, to which the Scriptures bear witness and which has been handed down in the Church by the power of the Holy Spirit, then the BEM reception process will become a process of mutual spiritual enrichment between the churches as they move forward to visible unity.

The reception of BEM involves at one and the same time a process of self-emptying and enrichment. The consultation thus recommended the churches of Europe to use BEM as a basis for dialogue between the different Christian traditions.

The third consultation in Görlitz (GDR), 25-28 June 1985, will deal with "The influence of historical, political and economic factors on the reception of BEM," and the last consultation in London (England), 18-22 November 1985, with "A credible reception of BEM in the churches at every level of their understanding, worship and practice."[16]

---

[16]Montreal 1963, Section 2 Report, p. 50.

The Orthodox participation in this series of consultations is very significant and of great value, not only because of Orthodox presence in each consultation but also because of Orthodox presentations. At the end of the four consultations the CEC plans to issue a volume based on the findings.

The Present Situation

The Lima event (1982) and the document on "Baptism, Eucharist and Ministry" have caused considerable turmoil in the life of all our churches, including the Orthodox Churches, and in their theological concerns. But why should this be? As one scientist has said: The important thing in research is to state the problem properly. The answer to this question is in fact very simple and it is of some significance for the whole history of the ecumenical movement because, for the first time in that history, the WCC member churches are facing the delicate and difficult question of how far they can receive a document which does not emanate from their own tradition. In other words, they are facing the problem of the reception of the Lima document.

The theological "imbroglio" caused by this new phenomenon has been dominating the life of our churches for the past three years. It must be said, however, that a considerable number of churches have given quite a positive response, though they have not been sparing in their criticisms, or have even in some cases indulged in an excess of triumphalism. Still others continue to regard the document with suspicion; Orthodox Churches probably fall into the latter category.

Whereas in some European churches, for instance in Germany and Britain, or also in the United States, BEM has not only become part of daily life but also figures in the programs of their theological faculties and ecumenical institutes, in the Orthodox world the document is still largely *terra incognita*—a *mysterion,* something which is not to be touched, or at best a matter for the specialists.

It has also become clear that although BEM has been translated into various non-European languages, it has not penetrated to all the corners of the world. As regards its geographical distribution, therefore, BEM is, at least for the time being, a concern of "First World" theologians.

Let us return to the present situation in the Orthodox world. This is entirely understandable, for BEM and its reception pose, and will continue to pose, a great dilemma for our churches—as indeed they do for other churches, too. The fact is that, despite the theological convergences contained in the Lima texts, the Orthodox Churches will never be able to accept them in their entirety. This opinion is shared by many Orthodox theologians who were involved in one way or another in the work on BEM before or after 1982.

On the other hand, there is no need for our churches to fear the text or decline to have anything to do with it. The role that the Orthodox Churches have to play in the future of BEM is as important and significant as the part they played in the preparatory period. All the churches are waiting anxiously and with interest to see what position the Orthodox Church will adopt in regard to the BEM texts.

Moreover, the Orthodox Church is one of the churches which sowed the seeds from which ecumenism was born. If it were now to become a fierce opponent of BEM, it could very well destroy the whole future of theological ecumenism. As we all know, the BEM text is not an Orthodox, nor a Catholic, nor a Protestant document, and no confession can recognize itself in it completely. Nor can we simply judge the document in terms of our particular confessional vocabulary and schemes of thought, for to do so would inevitably mean to misjudge it. John Gartshore, a churchman who takes a very critical stand on BEM, affirms that "no one church is going to find in it an exact description of its beliefs and practices; on the other hand few churches are likely to reject it out of hand saying 'our beliefs and practices cannot be accomodated by this statement' . . . "[17]

BEM and Ecclesiology

BEM is a convergence text in which the different communites, though still separated, can recognize themselves as part of the apostolic faith. In studying BEM we can trace the line of development, starting from mutual recognition between the churches and moving through spiritual emulation and fruitful confrontation in the quest for and defense of the truth as experienced by each of them separately, to the present period of theological consensus.

The theological consensus which BEM represents reflects the present state of the conciliar ecclesial community as it moves towards full realization. It echoes it on the theological level. Without trying to be a new confession or claiming to take the place of existing ecclesiologies, nor to be a full dogmatic exposition of a doctrine of baptism, eucharist and the ministry, the consensus document nevertheless summarizes what the churches can confess together, recognizing that they share the common tradition of the Gospel. It does so using a method which springs from the experience within that conciliar community and which is therefore positive, reconciliatory and comprehensive in its approach. The ecclesiology underlying BEM thus applies the formula of Montreal (1963) according to which we live in the tradition of the Gospel,

---

[17]J. Gartshore, "Chalcedon, Lambeth, the Covenant, Lima: What Next?," in *Reform,* (magazine of the United Reformed Church, UK), January, 1985.

the one source of life in the Church which binds Scripture and Tradition inseparably together. What ecclesiology is BEM based on?

It is difficult to take this question very far. This is why BEM is based on an apparently catholicizing ecclesiology, in the theological sense of the term, and it is why this underlying tendency is implicitly present though not explicitly defined in scholastic terms, at the start of all the different aspects of BEM. The Church is conceived as the ecclesial *koinonia,* based on biblical images and in a charismatic, eucharistic, prophetic and eschatological perspective.[18]

Sacramental life and the Word are the fruits, the expression, the result of its ecclesial community and at the same time they are its essential constitutive elements. Without the ecclesial prerequisites there are no sacraments, without the life of the sacraments and the prophetic Word there is no Church.

In all of this we find the elements of the Church's life, proclamation, mission, worship, eschatologial vision, presence in the world—sacraments and prophecy, confession and diakonia. The Church is the community of the New Covenant between God and his people (*laos*);[19] at the same time, it is the body of Christ and the people of God, that is, a community made up of those who are baptized in the name of the Trinity;[20] it is communion with God,[21] being itself called to proclaim and prefigure the kingdom of God by announcing the Gospel to the world and by its very existence as the body of Christ, and to bring a foretaste of the joy and glory of God's kingdom;[22] the Church receives this foretaste through the Holy Spirit in the eucharist,[23] the life of the new creation so that it may present to the world the image of a new humanity;[24] Christ is always the source of its mission and the foundation of its unity.[25]

However, the ecclesiology which underlies BEM is at the same time the basis of the consensus, in that it affirms that the apostolic tradition of the Gospel inevitably precedes any particular reflection on the texts.

---

[18]N. Nissiotis, *Foi et Constitution. Une communauté théologique de consensus (à la lumière du texte de Foi et Constitution: Baptême, Eucharistie, Ministere), in: Baptême, Eucharistie, Ministère—Une étape décisive vers l'unité chrétienne?,* Université de Geneve, Faculté Autonome de Théologie Protestante, Samedis de la Faculté, Janvier-Février, 1984, p. 12.

[19]Cf. BEM: B 1; E 17.

[20]E 19.

[21]M 1.

[22]M 4.

[23]E 18.

[24]M 19.

[25]M 12.

Besides, this is the only possible vision for BEM—an ecclesial community, with a trinitarian, christocentric and strongly pneumatological basis which is evident in its liturgical life and in its evangelical and missionary action in and for the world (*kosmos*) and in its emphasis on doxology and eschatology.

The consensus cannot be shaken by any discussions within this ecclesiological phenomenon of BEM. Indeed, if they are conducted in the interests of the community of consensus, they may well prove to be both important and fruitful. This can be illustrated by the difficulties the texts have in relation to certain traditional doctrines which continue to divide the confessions and demand a new approach if we are to reach a new consensus in the future. As affirmed in the preface of BEM, consensus is understood as "that experience of life and articulation of faith necessary to realize and maintain the Church's visible unity."[26]

Reception, Response or Rejection?

It is quite clear, and this is very important to note, that there has been a misunderstanding in many churches as to the meaning of reception, and particularly reception of the Lima document for today.

The Orthodox Church is among those in this uncomfortable position. There are different voices to be heard in the Orthodox world as to how the reception of BEM is to be understood. Theological opinion varies widely. This, in my view, is not entirely the fault of certain churches and it would have been advisable, before the publication of the Lima texts, to study and clarify the notion of reception as it applies to an ecumenical document such as BEM. An introduction of the type contained in BEM is certainly not enough to dispel the ambigious attitudes of the churches in relation to this burning but very significant issue.

Each church, and particularly the Orthodox Church, has a different conception of what reception means according to its tradition. There can be no question of using the term "reception" in relation to BEM in the same sense as the reception of the decisions of the ecumenical synods in the early centuries of the Church's history. Indeed this is not what the WCC is asking for. We are dealing here with an entirely new and different form of reception—the "ecumenical reception," if one may put it that way, of a convergence document which does not belong to any one tradition. This calls for "theological" reflection by all church members and above all for the celebration of the common faith. For the Orthodox themselves the reception of BEM is a

---

[26]BEM, Preface, 9.

tremendous opportunity to rediscover the essence of Orthodoxy,[27] not in a confessional sense, but as the common tradition in which all the churches meet and which is the basis for their historical responses and their practical witness.

1. Reception in its Classical Form

Reception is also part of the ongoing life of the Church. Ever since the time of our Lord and the Apostles, the Church constantly *receives* and *re-receives* the message of our Lord. In fact, one can go even further back and make the point that *our Lord himself* received not only vertically (καθέτως) the mission from his Father, but also horizontally (ὁριζοντίως) the history of the people of Israel to which he belonged as Man.[28]

Thus, the idea of reception precedes the Church itself and it must be underlined that in a very deep sense the Church *was born* out of an ongoing process of reception; the Church itself is a product of reception.

But in spite of this general sense of reception—which we must always bear in mind—the term, in the course of history, acquired a very specific and technical sense. This sense is mainly associated with the *councils* of the Church and by the *decision-making* of the Fathers. It entered even into the terminology of canon law and acquired there a special meaning: it is the acceptance and consent given by the people to a particular conciliar or ecclesiological decision. In the present times the conception and the idea of reception become a basic theological *concept* in the ecumenical context.

It is also important to understand that the term "reception" of the Lima document is not already the "end" (τέλος) of the ecumenical pilgrimage towards a true and full communion of the Christian families. BEM is intended to initiate a new dynamism. It does this by being a *sign* which stands at the main crossroads of the ecumenical task and this sign—visible from everywhere—is such that there will be no escape.

As Jean Tillard affirms, "Everybody who seriously comes and works for the ecumenical movement has to look upon this theological convergence as a 'way ahead' of God's people."[29]

A significant difficulty is also the last part of this document which raises quite an important point: the language problem which does not

---

[27]I. Bria, "La réception du BEM. Une orientation théologique orthodoxe," in *Baptême, Eucharistie, Ministère—Une étape décisive vers l'unité chrétienne?*, p. 70.

[28]J. Zizioulas, "The Theological Problem of 'Reception'," in *Centro Pro Unione*, (Fall, 1984) 3.

[29]J. M. R. Tillard OP, "BEM: The Call for a Judgment upon the Churches and the Ecumenical Movement, in *Mid-Stream*, 23, no. 3 (July, 1984) 234.

exactly facilitate reception will have to be tackled. We fully realize that this is not an easy problem and we also know that the Commission is aware of it. Indeed, the preface indicates that the language of the text is not the language of today and that the document "will likely stimulate many reformulations of the text into the varied languages of our time."[30] But the language problem does not arise only in terms of past and present, but also between the different forms of expression used in theological-ecclesial themes within the churches of today.

For example, in the Greek translation of the document a term is chosen in the title itself which—according to my view—does not properly reflect the intention of the convergence statements on "Ministry" and would certainly not bring forward an immediately favorable reaction among many of our Protestant brethren. The term "ministry" (amt, in the German equivalent "office") is here rendered by the Greek word *hierosyne (ἱερωσύνη)* There is of course a word in the Greek language corresponding to "ministry" (amt = office): *leitourgema (λειτούργημα), arhe (ἀρχή), yperesia (ὑπηρεσία),* etc.

But when one of these terms is used, it bears no theological-ecclesial relation to what is meant in the document. If *hierosyne* is used, however, only one aspect of "ministry" is covered, an aspect that is certainly referred to in the document but which is not only referred to in the title or in the chapter on the subject, i.e. ordained priestly ministry. The term "ministry" (amt = office) suggests something much broader, more diverse and even ambigious.

Professor Konidaris translates "ministry—office" (amt) for example as "leitourgema" (λειτούγημα) followed in brackets by *hierosyne.*[31] And if he is writing in his study in Greek about *hierosyne* in relation to the Lima document, he uses "priestly ministry—priestly office" in brackets.[32]

I have given this striking example in order to show that the theological-ecclesiological background of each church plays a major role which must not be overlooked in relation to reception.

It is precisely for this reason that the convergence document represents a stimulus and a challenge to sustained work on the language and the historical background of the language, on thought-forms and

---

[30]BEM, Preface, 9.

[31]G. Konidaris, *For the Problem of the Unity of the Churches. Is a Symphony for Liturgima (Hierosyne) and Eucharist in the Ecumenical Movement Possible?* (Athens, 1978) (in Greek).

[32]Ibid., p. 8; see also G. Larentzakis, *The Convergence Statement on Baptism, Eucharist and Ministry of the Faith and Order Commission as a Stimulus to the Work of the Churches,* paper prepared for 2nd BEM Consultation, Conference of European Churches, Iserlohn, FRG (10-14 December, 1984), p. 7 (German version).

also on the non-theological and non-ecclesial factors in the different churches so that we can better understand our Christian brethren either by retaining differences of language where it is clear that the same thing is meant or by means of a new language expressing what has been jointly worked out and understood, even if this involves an unfamiliar terminology.

2. Response

A first major step proposed in Vancouver 1983 was an evaluation of the doctrinal results through the reception process of BEM by the churches. Thus we read in the Vancouver Report:

> It is also important to disinguish the 'process of reception' and the 'official response.' The 'official response,' which is requested at a relatively early date, is intended to initiate a process of study and communication in which each church will attempt to provide an answer to the four preface questions, answers which are not simply the response of individuals or groups within the church but which, in some sense, understood by the church itself, are given on behalf of the church. This 'official response' is explicitly not understood to be the church's ultimate decisions about 'Baptism, Eucharist, and Ministry,' but rather the initial step in a longer process of reception. This 'process of reception' is something which each church will have to understand in terms of its own tradition . . . [33]

"By way of concrete illustration," we take this example from the Lutheran Lazareth who affirms categorically that "it means that you do not go home and measure Lima in terms of the Council of Trent or the Augsburg Confession or the Thirty-Nine Articles. We are reversing the order and asking, 'How do you validate your communion's articulation of its faith in light of the *paradosis* of the *kerygma,* the holy tradition of the Gospel?' So, for example, if there is any incompatibility between BEM and the fifth article of the Augsburg Confession on 'the Ministry,' it may be so much the worse for the Augsburg Confession."[34]

Reception and Response—Some Examples

Several responses to BEM show that some of the churches can

---

[33]D. Gill (ed.), *Gathered for Life. Official Report VI Assembly, World Council of Churches, Vancouver/Canada, 24 July—10 August, 1983,* (Geneva/Grand Rapids, 1983); "Taking Steps Towards Unity," pp. 45-47.

[34]W. H. Lazareth, "Baptism, Eucharist and Ministry Updated," in *Journal of Ecumenical Studies,* 21, no. 1 (1984) 16.

distinguish between what is meant by an initial *response,* before the end of 1985, and a *reception* of the document, which will take longer. Thus the Lutheran Church in America states:

> The request of the Faith and Order Commission to the churches is twofold. The first involves a process of receiving, *reception.* It includes all the phases and aspects of a process by which a church makes the results of an ecumenical dialogue or statement a part of its faith and life. Reception thus is a process involving all parts of the church, all believers. It may take years and it only occurs as Christ graciously accomplishes it by his *Baptism, Eucharist and Ministry* in the sense of the term "reception."

> The second fold of the Commission's request involves an official response. This is what this convention is being asked to do. Such a response may be seen as part of the process leading to reception, but it is not be identified with reception. The response offered here assumes that *Baptism, Eucharist and Ministry* is a unique document.

And the draft response of the Church of Scotland (Reformed):

> 'Response' is only one of the two reactions to the document which the Faith and Order Commission invites from the churches. The other is 'reception.' 'Response' is asked for by the end of 1985; but 'reception' will continue for many years after this initial response this year. As churches discern and work out the practical consequences which their responses entail for their relations with other churches, they will be swept beyond mere endorsement of a text: they will enter upon a process of receiving other churches as churches—Rom 15.5: 'Receive you one another as Christ also received us.' Reception of this kind is what the ecumenical movement exists to promote. Only when we are a little way along this road can we arrive at a really just and of course not uncritical appreciation of what the churches are saying.

Finally the draft of the Church of England:

> We note that the question does not ask whether we can recognize in the text the faith of Anglicanism. It would therefore not be appropriate simply to compare what the text says with the historical formularies of the Church of England. We understand that the phrasing of the questions directs us to consider how far the Lima text reflects the apostolic faith of the universal Church: that is that

faith which is "uniquely revealed in the holy Scriptures and set forth in the catholic creeds, which faith the Church is called upon to proclaim fresh in each general" (The Declaration of Assent. The Canons of the Church of England, Canon C 15). The question asked of us involves the identification and affirmation of the universal Christian tradition which has been mediated to us through the various traditions of all our churches."[35]

BEM Needs Discernment and Humility . . .

This document is the outcome of long years of devoted work by many people. It has been prepared and drafted by theologians from various WCC member churches.

Should certain churches, and I think in particular of the Orthodox Church, decide to reject the document outright and adopt a totally negative position without making a critical analysis of the whole text and considering what purpose it might serve for others, the whole Orthodox contribution to the ecumenical movement would be endangered. For this document can serve as a good theological instrument which is helpful not only for others but also to some extent for Orthodoxy itself.

Orthodox participation in the emergence of BEM has been considerable from the outset, and on more than one occasion eminent Orthodox theologians have contributed significantly to the process. The Orthodox have thus not only been present but have also made a deep theological contribution. Among the many aspects of BEM which have benefited from Orthodox theology and bear the 'mark' of Orthodoxy the following may be mentioned:

On the question of Scripture and Tradition, BEM was helped by the presence of the Orthodox who were able to make their theological position understood effectively. As regards the relationship to Scripture, Orthodox theologians have always taken the biblical texts seriously, though not slipping into a simplistic biblicism,[36] and see the sacraments as being esentially instituted by the words of Christ himself: the commission to baptize as contained in the Gospel of Matthew (28.18-20), the accounts in the synoptic Gospels of the paschal Eucharist of Christ and the tradition reported by Paul (1 Cor 11.23-26) on the subject of the ordained ministry. They fought to have the tradition of the laying on of hands with the invocation of the Holy Spirit as attested

---

[35]M. Thurian, *Observations on the Emerging Evaluation of BEM,* FO/85:13 (March, 1985), pp. 3-4.

[36]M. Thurian, *Quelle est la contribution spécifique de l'Orthodoxie au BEM?* (Paper delivered at Chambésy Seminar) 1 May, 1985, p. 6.

to in the letters to Timothy (1 Tim 4.14, 2 Tim 1.6) recognized by others as apostolic, fundamental and necessary.

Another instance of Orthodox participation in BEM was their insistence that the great Tradition of the early centuries of the Church, the patristic, liturgical and conciliar Tradition, be duly considered. I have mentioned only a small sample of the Orthodox theological contributions but in all the "shining stones" which make up the interconfessional "mosaic" of the different traditions represented in BEM, there is a clear return to the apostolic and patristic Tradition which is due also to the Orthodox contribution. Therefore, some Protestants even accuse BEM of being too Orthodox, but this is a false assessment.

The BEM texts need to be considered and studied with discernment and humility. A century of history cannot be wiped out and denied by a decision taken perhaps without thought to the consequences of the future.

Orthodoxy is well placed to help with BEM and to use it more as an instrument for ecumenical dialogue.[37] Through the texts and the commentaries, which admittedly sometimes seem to make the texts complicated, and the language which may not be easy and familiar to everybody, Orthodoxy can put over their message to the others. The difficulty in speaking about reception in connection with the Faith and Order Commission's statements is made clear by the Roman Catholic Professor Peter Neuner when he says: "There is great perplexity on all sides as to how reception is possible or what it signifies. This applies also to the Lima paper of the WCC. Here the difficulties are perhaps even greater than with other comparable texts because the literary form and style of this document is far from being uniform."[38] BEM is a crossroads of theological convergence where the Orthodox Churches are trying to harmonize the process leading to the visible unity of the Church.

Lastly, while Orthodox may not expect much of BEM, it is nevertheless true that there can be no BEM without Orthodoxy.

BEM has not been concluded; Lima marked not the goal but the beginning of a long and even more difficult road. BEM still has a long way to go towards a future theological consensus. However, the

---

[37] A. P. F. Sell, "Responding to Baptism, Eucharist and Ministry: A Word to the Reformed Churches," in *Studies from the World Alliance of Reformed Churches* 3 (1984) 4.

[38] P. Neuner, "Konvergenzen im Verständnis des geistlichen Amtes—Möglichkeiten der Rezeption." Eine katholische Überlegung zum Amts-Papier der Konvergenzerklärungen der Kommission für Glauben und Kirchenverfassunt des ÖRK, in *Una Sancta,* 38 (1983) 198.

reception process will confirm the fact that the WCC member churches are at a stage of convergence which, in my opinion, goes beyond the stage of bilateral theological dialogue. It is understandable that there are some frustrations, certain limits at every stage along the way to visible unity, but there is also a certain amount of freedom. The important thing is to keep an adequate dialogue going at every stage. The churches of the West, Catholic and Protestant, defined their faith and doctrine without dialogue with the East, in a climate of schism and polemic. Nowadays all the churches must reject this non-dialogical attitude inherited from the past. This is why, in formulating their answers, Orthodoxy cannot be content to say *yes* or *no* to this or that section, but should prepare theological desiderata to send to the World Council of Churches in order to continue the dialogue. The problems emanating from BEM can then be treated in a different perspective. We very much hope that in the experience of the reception process all the churches will be able to build one another up and understand one another better, to their mutual enrichment. But this does not automatically guarantee that the reception process will not develop a negative dynamic, and it will be for all of us to safeguard against that.

A last very important point should also be mentioned: BEM is not isolated from the other theological study projects of Faith and Order. The study "Towards the Common Expression of the Apostolic Faith Today" and the study "The Unity of the Church and the Renewal of Human Community" closely relate to each other. BEM, apostolic faith, and unity/renewal—all three are asking for mutual theological support and serious reflection; BEM cannot exist without the other two studies.

Through the Lima texts Christians can as it were discover the essential things that *unite* them at this stage of the ecumenical movement and which should also make them *one* because the future of humankind depends on the restoration of Christian unity and the reconciliation between Christians.[39]

But, as one spiritual father has said, "Wherever there is human will, the grace and blessing of God are manifest." Let us pray that this symposium will develop in this way with the guidance of the Holy Spirit.

---

[39]N. Zernov, "The Reintegration of the Christian Community and the Ecumenical Movement," in *Pro-Regno—Pro Sanctuario* (Nijkerk, Holland, 1950), p. 541.

The Meaning of Reception in Relation to the Results of Ecumenical Dialogue on the Basis of the Faith and Order Document "Baptism, Eucharist and Ministry"

NIKOS A. NISSIOTIS

THE DOCUMENT *Baptism, Eucharist and Ministry* (hereafter referred to as BEM), represents in many respects an important phase of development within the ongoing ecumenical movement and dialogue as shaped and carried out by the fellowship of churches of the World Council of Churches (WCC). The text introduces new approaches to the debate over dogmatic differences in the three main doctrinal issues of ecclesiology. Apart from this, it attempts to formulate what the churches can confess together, using as their criterion the Scriptures and their experience in the one apostolic faith. BEM is proposing—with the agreement of the representatives of churches in the WCC plus the Roman Catholic Church which, exceptionally, is a member of the Faith and Order Commission—to be "received" by the churches, and then to be studied and commented upon by them.

One hopes that such study and comments and, eventually a critical response to the Faith and Order Secretariat, will be made on the basis of this act of "reception." This concept introduces a new factor in the ecumenical movement but also reminds us, at the same time, of one of the most crucial and significant acts of the universal Church throughout the centuries. There is a notorious difference between this ancient church tradition of "reception" and today's request in the context of the ongoing ecumenical dialogue in basic matters of the ecclesial faith. Still, this request marks the beginning of a new stage in serious and consistent church-centered ecumenism insofar as, on the one hand, it reflects the progress achieved in the ecumenical dialogue on doctrinal issues and, on the other, because the text of BEM itself reflects the preliminary consensus reached upon these issues within the one apostolic faith.

Thus the "Lima text" of BEM, with its remarkable extent of agreed doctrinal statements, has been proposed by the governing bodies of the WCC to the churches for "reception." Though "new" to a certain extent in methodology, language and its approach to the ages-old disputed ecclesiological issues, BEM should not be regarded as exceptional or entirely new. BEM stands in consistent continuity with the fundamental principles and premises, as well as intention and scope, of the whole ecumenical movement as it has been represented and embodied by the WCC thorugh the Faith and Order movement. At the same time it presupposes the scheme of church reunions already realized, as well as the agreements reached by contemporary bilateral or multilateral dialogues between separated church traditions and confessions.

One must study carefully the published documents from such dialogues in order to appreciate the "parenthood" of the convergences in BEM, and in the agreed statements on the same topics in the official report of the Roman Catholic/Orthodox dialogue on the mystery of the Church and the Eucharist in the light of the Holy Trinity (Munich, 1982). Based on a trinitarian, and especially a pneumatological approach, this represents an identity of opinions on the crucial issues of ecclesiology.[1] See also the extremely successful official documents on the ministry by Roman Catholic and Orthodox theologians (Chambésy, 1978).[2] We can mention also the agreements produced by the Old Catholic/Orthodox conversations on the doctrine of God (1975), christology (1977), and ecclesiology (1981), as well as the progressive rapprochement between European Protestants and Lutherans on delicate issues like the Word of God and the tradition of the Church, the meaning of sacraments, etc. (e.g., the most recent meeting in Kavalla, Greece, 1984), and those between the Moscow Patriarchate and the same Lutheran Church. One should refer also to other bilateral dialogues and their reports, especially to one which is very interesting for the Orthodox, i.e., the Final Report of the Anglican/Roman Catholic International Commission (ARCIC). This presents an extraordinary consensus on old controversial issues of ecclesiology, especially on the nature of the Eucharist (about which we read: "The agreement is offered as a consensus at the level of faith so that all of us might be able to say . . . This is the Christian faith of the Eucharist"), but also on ministry and ordination, on authority in the Church (including

---

[1] The full text in *Episkepsis,* 277 (1982), pp. 12-20.

[2] Published in *Episkepsis,* 183 (1978), pp. 7-13.

the delicate issue of papal authority and infallibility). The report also expresses completely new, constructive approaches on both sides and with a view to future further elaboration.[3] Moreover, we can refer to the Anglican/Lutheran Conversations (Pullach Report, 1972), Lutheran/Roman Catholic Conversations (Malta, 1972; the Eucharist, 1978; Ways to Community, 1980; All Under One Christ, 1980; The Ministry in the Church, 1981, etc.), to the Reformed/Baptist Conversations (Report, 1977), to the Roman Catholic/Disciples of Christ Dialogue (Report, 1981), to the Roman Catholic/Methodist Conversations (Denver, 1971; Dublin, 1976; Honolulu Reports, 1981), to the Roman Catholic/Reformed Church Conversations (The Presence of Christ in Church and World, 1977), etc.[4]

Therefore the request of the WCC Faith and Order Commission for "reception" of BEM is addressed to the churches only and expecially because this text represents the agreement already reached among the churches. Thus BEM is not an isolated text but reflects the results of ecumenical dialogues among this fellowship of churches—a "fellowship" which of course is still on the way to achieving conciliar fellowship, and has no ecclesial nature of its own. At the same time BEM is not simply another document of the WCC, such as are often sent to the churches for information and exchange of views, or for taking a common stand in current problems of church life on the church's missionary or social involvement. BEM is the fruit of long and strenuous work by Faith and Order, which right at the beginning of its existence, in Lausanne in 1927, had stated in its first conference report: "Notwithstanding the differences in doctrine amongst us we are united in a common Christian faith which is proclaimed in the Holy Scriptures and is witnessed to and safeguarded in the ecumenical creed, commonly called the Nicene, and in the apostles' creed, whose faith is continuously confirmed in the spiritual experience of the Church of Christ."[5]

Thus it is clear that Faith and Order intended not only to state that "we are united in a common Christian Faith," but to emphasize that this faith is "continuously confirmed in the spiritual experience of the Church of Christ." There is something "more" meant with these words

---

[3] See *Towards a Church of England Response to BEM and ARCIC,* (London, 1985), pp. 65-102.

[4] For all of these conversations one may consult *Growth in Agreement: Reports and Agreed Statements of Ecumenical Conversations on a World Level,* ed. Harding Meyer and Lukas Vischer (New York, 1982), pp. 1-504, as well as a kind of advanced, new joint catechism between separated churches in the West: *Neues Glaubensbuch, Der gemeinsame christliche Glaube.* Hrsg. von J. Feiner and L. Vischer. Freiburg, (Zurich, 1973), pp. 1-660.

[5] *A Documentary History of the Faith and Order Movement. 1927-1963,* section 4, para. 28, ed. L. Vischer (St. Louis, 1963), p. 33.

than simple theological comparative work, theological investigations, exchange of information or even church negotiations on doctrinal matters. Faith and Order envisaged, ultimately, taking account of the whole of church life and spirituality as it pursued its main goal: to help the churches to regain their visible unity. It is self-evident, therefore, that Faith and Order would eventually have to engage its member churches in profound ecclesiological study, and follow their corporate progress as they sought to redefine their apostolic faith. Consequently Faith and Order's request for "reception" is one of the signs and results of its authentic work towards an ecclesial reunion.

Furthermore one must notice an additional factor which makes the request for "reception" both necessary and consistent. This is the fact that this document has been produced by the Commission on Faith and Order *together with* the churches. Because the text had been sent to them in draft form in 1974 for their "response," BEM is a paper written with the churches, with their involvement, and with their comments and criticisms. The churches have involved themselves with this statement more than any other, and to some extent they have come to regard it as something of their own work, ecumenism and faith. It is also important that when we say "churches" we mean here all of the churches, including the Roman Catholic Church, whose theologians were involved in elaborating the text. Catholic theologians themselves refer to this exxceptional situation as giving the Lima document a special significance. Jean Tillard, O.P., has written, "Consequently BEM is more than a document of the World Council of Churches. It is—thanks to the Council and through one of its principal commissions—a document of the whole ecumenical movement. This distinction is very important."[6]

The request for "reception" signifies that "Christian churches have reached a new level of convergence."[7] The "reception" of an important doctrinal text can be the result only of an advanced stage of ecumenical dialogue. It recalls the perspective of the church's ultimate conciliar fellowship; thus it is a kind of nostalgic remembrance of one of the fundamental characteristics of the apostolic Church in those past ages when church unity prevailed over heresies and schisms. Thus it reflects the desire of local churches for a double relationship, first to the one catholic-universal Church of which they are a part, and second to each other as church communities which are mutually renewed and strengthened by their common sharing in the apostolic tradition.

---

[6] Jean M. R. Tillard, O.P., "BEM: A Call for a Judgement upon the Churches and the Ecumenical Movement," *Mid-Stream,* 23, no. 3 (July, 1984) 234.

[7] Jeffrey Gros, "Baptism, Eucharist and Ministry: Introduction," *Journal of Ecumenical Studies,* 21, no. 1 (Winter, 1984) 2.

1. "Reception"—an ecclesiological interpretation on the basis of Scripture and Tradition

What is meant by "reception" in the Preface of the BEM document is certainly *not* identical with the term "reception" as applied to the decisions of the ancient ecumenical synods of the Church on a universal scale, before the schisms of the eleventh and sixteenth centuries. There are, however, some factors in the Bible, and in the praxis of the ancient churches which "received" the decisions of the ecumenical synods, which point to the common origins and purposes of these two different kinds of "reception."

Christian faith is principally a "receiving" event. It is centered either around the revelatory event in Christ, as God giving himself to man in order to be received by him (as is evident in the sacramental life, especially in the Eucharist, which is an act of God's offering his communion and man receiving it), or around the Word of God, which is to be "heard" and accepted by the believer. Faith is, in its nature, a receiving act, denoting a dependence of man upon the grace of God.

The Scriptures return again and again to this fundamental aspect of faith as a giving-receiving-thanksgiving, dialogical relationship between the triune God and man. John Zizioulas notes that Paul illustrates this truth by reminding his readers that they have received Jesus Christ (Col 2.6), and that he himself has first received the Gospel (1 Cor 15.1, Gal 1.9-12) and then "handed on" that which he received (especially in connection with the Eucharist, 1 Cor 11.33).[8] This implies the obligation of *all* the faithful to "hand on" what they have received to others (2 Tim 2.2). In this process of "reception" in the biblical sense, there is neither compulsion or domination, nor a blind submission or obligation on the part either of God (the giver) or of man (the receiver). The *act* of reception is the operation of the Holy Spirit communicating, in full freedom, the grace given by Christ to all persons whom he wants to save, on the basis of their free decision. Evangelism and mission are the outcome of this free exchange, this giving and receiving without any sense of faith "imposing herself but rather offering herself to the world for reception."

In the biblical context one can further remark that "reception" is to be understood in the light of the trinitarian God as a koinonia of persons. Thus "reception" concerns distinctive persons among the faithful, but views them as members of the church community. It implies a personal decision to appropriate faith and grace as the *apostolic* faith, i.e., "reception" is a communal event which comes through the community of the historical Church. The Roman Catholic theologian Richard

---

[8] John Zizioulas, "The Theological Problem of Reception," in *Centro Pro Unione*, 26 (Fall 1984) 4.

Stewart writes: "Reception concerns our response to the Word, our making our own the Tradition, the apostolic faith."[9] It is, therefore, a communal event both as giving and as receiving, and it is through reception that one belongs to the divine communion and the human community of faith. It is these which give one's life its ultimate meaning. "Reception" presupposes a communal act and leads to community.

Furthermore it empowers persons, as members of distinct communities of faith, to envisage and realize together the communion of the one Church, a communion which is experienced in local churches as they are reaffirmed by this process of giving-receiving the one faith by the one Spirit.[10]

It is on this basis in the Bible and the apostolic Church that "reception" became a crucial ecclesial act with a specific ecclesiological meaning: that local churches "receive" decisions on the basis of love and freedom and not of power and domination of their higher authoritative bodies, and above all of ecumenical synods speaking about the development and clarification of doctrine and of church life. "Reception," then, appears to be a one-way traffic *from* above, from the dignitaries and the hierarchialized church structures *to* the people of God in the local church. In reality, however, "reception" in the historical life of the Church operates on the basis of this biblical-ecclesiological tradition of a *communal* origin, a communal transmission, and a communal reality of reception. It is in the light of the apostolic principle that "it pleased the Apostles and elders with the whole Church" (Acts 15.22). It intends to strengthen, develop and confirm the local church as part of the universal, catholic Church in realizing its vocation to become, through reception of the truth, the communion with and in God of all of those who believe in him by the same act of faith. That is why, speaking of communion in relationship with the operation of reception, one can observe that "evangelical koinonia is neither an unattainable ideal nor the peculiar vocation of some specific groups of baptized people. It is what all the churches have to achieve together to be honest to God."[11]

The important thing to notice is that "the factual reception in the ancient Church was conditioned by the fact that each local church is truly church and so can speak to the other churches and for the other churches since all live from the same Spirit who guides the decisions."[12]

---

[9] Richard Stewart, "What do the Churches do with Ecumenical Agreements?" *Centro Pro Unione,* 25 (Spring, 1894) 2.

[10] John Zizioulas adds on this matter that "not any form of community is ecclesial community," i.e., it is not "ecclesial community" if it lacks the one apostolic faith which it should both receive and transmit.

[11] J. Tillard, "BEM," p. 237.

[12] Edward Kilmartin, *Journal of Ecumenical Studies,* 21 (1984), p. 48.

It has been said that "reception" is a relatively modern term to describe an ancient process by which a theological doctrine or decision of a council is acknowledged as valid by a local church or the Church universal.[13] "Reception" in its classical meaning and praxis presupposes the reality of the Church universal as Catholic, and that the Church professes an interpretation of its doctrine through its representative councils. These councils mediate the operation of the Holy Spirit upon those gathered at the same place with one accord—i.e., in the Council—and those who receive conciliar decisions, i.e., the local churches as parts of the Church universal. It is precisely this presupposition, of course, which has been shaken in modern times by the schismatic church situation.

That is why in ancient times the process of reception occurred with remarkable simplicity, without requiring juridically normative bodies apart from those already functioning in a spiritual and pastoral way: the synods of bishops expressing the highest authority, which is the consciousness of the Church as catholic (i.e., both universal and local). As Liviu Stan writes, "Reception occurred, sooner or later spontaneously, not in an organized way with juridical forms of directives and by no means through a sort of general plebiscite. What is involved is rather another sort of plebiscite, which has its origin in the action of the Holy Spirit."[14]

2. Reception in modern dialogical-ecumenical meaning

The term "reception," therefore, in contemporary ecumenical language should be understood in a way which is different, but which was not entirely absent from the meaning and praxis of the ancient Church of the ecumenical councils. In ancient times also "reception" did not happen automatically, as a result of a one-way movement "from above." Various councils were convened, but only seven were acknowledged as ecumenical. There are different types and processes of reception depending on what the local or universal church is invited to "receive"; there is a difference, for example, between receiving doctrines and "receiving" specific decisions about church life professed by canon law at a particular time. Thus we know that many canons voted by ecumenical councils were quietly modified or negated by the local churches, without this causing any trouble in the universal church community.

---

[13]Such wording was used by Commission members during the long process of shaping and re-shaping the Preface to BEM.

[14]*Concerning the Church Acceptance of the Decisions of Ecumenical Synods in Councils and the Ecumenical Movement, WCC Studies,* No. 5, p. 70.

In reality, "receiving" is not an instant decision, but rather a long process. There is a kind of "maturation" of suggested new elements accompanied by a two-fold judgment: a "critical" one, testing whether what has been received is in harmony with the apostolic faith as this Church has received it, and a "practical" one, asking, "What should be done in and between the churches involved if they have found this faith context acceptable?"[15] "Reception," therefore, is not a once-for-all, fixed dogmatic stance demanding a blind and uncritical acceptance. "Reception" means a definite endorsement of certain basic doctrines which are self-evident parts of the one apostolic faith. But it also means exchange, for their mutual benefit, among the churches of spiritual gifts of grace which might edify them in their struggle to define further truth, and to initiate new common action in mission and service in the world or find striking new ways of interpreting the same faith and order of the one apostolic faith.

Everyone, regardless of confessional adherence, can see the recent dramatic developments in the ecumenical dialogue, and especially the growing community of churches working towards a conciliar fellowship through common prayer, diaconia, and witness. From this perspective one can observe—while recognizing the distinctive meaning and praxis of "reception" in the ancient Church and as we use the term today— that "the traditional mode of reception is not out of date. It has simply been readjusted."[16] Within the "new" koinonia of the churches, although in a schismatic situation, the word "reception" points to the fundamental common sharing in the one apostolic faith as it has been handed down to us as communities of faith, communities struggling to reinterpret their common heritage with new language, new emphases and new insights but always with a converging ethos, attitude and intention which has been acquired by their experience with the one ecumenical movement.

There are, today, different modes of understanding and practicing "reception." This is due to the new church situation, which is neither that of the full communion and union of the ancient times (though, of course, there were local church bodies, or heretical groups, outside this communion right from the beginning of the historical life of the Church), nor that of total separation and polemic of the churches against each other. The ecumenical dialogue creates a new situation for understanding "reception" as co-edification, or mutual encouragement for the sake of the dynamic presence of the faith in a progressively de-Christianizing world, one which forces us to a common rethinking

---

[15]Richard Stewart, "Churches," p. 5.

[16]John Zizioulas, "The Theological Problem," p. 6.

of our one faith in Christ. This is especially true with the growing *fellowship* between the churches, as well as the formal schemes of church reunion and the bilateral dialogues as direct negotiations for re-establishing church unity.

We must be committed to remaining faithful to the Gospel and to our common apostolic tradition, to avoiding further centrifugal trends in our respective church communities, and must be open to further convergence. Given this, and applying this modern meaning of "reception," one can join in mutually receiving one another within the reality of the one apostolic faith. We do this by accepting new elements of interpretation in its expression—regardless of what particular church tradition we belong to. Concerning "new language," Richard Stewart reminds us that the essence of the act of faith for Roman Catholicism does not reside in terminology but in the essence of faith itself. He quotes Saint Thomas in his *Summa Theologiae:* "actus fidei non terminatur ad exuntiabile, sed ad rem." And concerning these "new insights," he quotes Vatican II, declaring that the Church must "constantly move forward towards the fullness of divine truth and with the help of the Holy Spirit . . . to a deeper realization and a clearer understanding of the unfathomable riches of Christ" (*Decr. Unitatis redintegratio*). In this connection he makes the pointed remark (as a Roman Catholic) that "we should not forget that the long period of division has not been empty or sterile."[17]

This long period of division amongst the churches is, indeed, not at all sterile and *only* negative for the renewal of church life and theology, especially ecclesiology. Thanks to the results of the ecumenical dialogue and of the ecumenical fellowship of churches in the WCC, we can cherish today a rich heritage of spiritual gifts of which BEM is their expression. This makes "reception" appear in a new meaning, a new form and praxis, as an ecclesial category of paramount importance for all churches struggling for the renewal of their life. Only in this way can we *benefit* from this period of simultaneous division (after the schism) and of ecumenical *dialogues.*

Thinking of "reception" on the basis of BEM and in relation to the results of ecumenical dialogue, it is remarkable how Roman Catholics view this document as a judgment upon the churches and the ecumenical movement insofar as "church communities are now confronted with new challenges . . . and a desire for profound reformation." They are "forced to look at the apostolic tradition with new eyes . . . " Because BEM is "an arrow at the crossroads pointing towards what has been discovered as the way to achieve this common faithfulness

---

[17]Richard Stewart, "Churches," p. 4.

and by receiving this document the churches decide to give priority to the desire of the Spirit of God over their own fears."[18] In this sense for Roman Catholiocs as well as others, the suggestion of BEM for "reception" becomes a challenge to *all* churches, "inviting them to elaborate that which we can say together . . . taking into consideration the other dialogues that a church can establish or has already established with the other churches" and that "because of the complexity of the notion of reception and in order to have a real reception of an ecumenical convergence and a declaration of an ecumenical consensus, it is the heart itself of the ecclesial life which must be reached."[19]

Reception, therefore, is implied by the converging elements that separated church communities can confirm together, in their ecumenical dialogue, as standing in the one apostolic faith. This kind of confirmation is not simply a scholastic-verbal one, but the concrete result of mutually-enriching emphases which are shared between the churches involved in ecumenical fellowship and dialogue. "The Baptist influence in the understanding of the theology of baptism is matched (in the BEM text) by an enriching Trinitarian pneumatological emphasis in the eucharist text contributed out of the riches of the Orthodox tradition . . . the community, which interprets church tradition is broadened so other aspects and riches of that tradition are brought into the picture, restoring balance and coherence to our understanding of our common tradition cradled in all our separated traditions."[20]

3. Reception as a process of receiving the experience of ecumenical dialogue

The real intention of the suggestion to present BEM for "reception" to the churches is not to have an immediate, full endorsement of the text as a kind of new common "confession" by the doctrinally-separated churches. That is why in the Preface of BEM this term "reception"—used in its modern meaning, in relation to the ongoing ecumenical dialogues—is clearly illustrated, developed and clarified by specifying, in four areas, what this "reception" means. These areas are first, whether the text makes us recognize the faith of the Church through the ages; second, the consequences of this text for inter-church relations and dialogues; third, the effect it can have in the actual life of the churches (worship-education-ethical and spiritual life and witness); and fourth, the suggestions that each church can offer for the

---

[18]J. Tillard, "BEM," pp. 236-38.

[19]E. Lanne, O.S.B., "Le probleme de la réception par les Eglises," *Oecumenisme,* 70 (1983) 33-34.

[20]Mary Tanner, "BEM and the Community of Men and Women Study," *Journal of Ecumenical Studies,* 21, no. 1 (1984) 244.

long-range research project "Towards the Common Expression of the Apostolic Faith."[21]

Thus it is evident that one speaks of "reception" as an act of recognition of something new that has happened, and is happening, among the churches as they converge towards the apostolic roots of their own faith. But this "recognition" means a new beginning for further growth together in the pre-suppositions and prerequisites for church unity by renewing church life, by applying the text in further ecumenical dialogues and finally by linking it with the next central topic of studies on the one apostolic faith. "Reception" here means a dynamic process of receiving and also bringing to life the spirit which is hidden behind the text, in order to advance towards unity through inner renewal, self-judgment and further commitment to the ecumenical dialogue.

By proposing "reception," the BEM text invites churches to move from their experience of ecumenical dialogue in the past, to affirm its value and importance, and to press towards new attempts in the same direction. Receiving, as a process, means that the doctrinal differences we have inherited from the past, and the differences which lead to special tensions for the Church in the contemporary world, should not be regarded as mutually exclusive for church communities engaged in different types of ecumenical dialogue. BEM appears to be both an effort to transcend the very old, violent struggles on crucial issues of ecclesiology by a maximum of common confessional statements in the areas of theory, praxis, liturgy, mission and service to the world and, at the same time, it opens a new horizon of further and more profound convergence on the way to "consensus" on matters of faith. This is "reception" as a receiving, dynamic process, a process not only of verbal confession but also, and mainly, of inner transformation and spriritual rehabilitation of church life in today's world. And this comes as a result of the growing church koinonia within the ecumenical movement.

That is why BEM has a particular significance at the present moment: it is offered to the churches for "reception" as a chrystalized form of their ecumenical experience. Consequently Lucas Vischer writes: "The texts are no longer merely the common opinions of an international and ecumenical commission of theologians, but already represent the result of extended discussion with the churches. Thus the process of reception has entered a second phase."[22]

---

[21] *Baptism, Eucharist and Ministry,* Faith and Order Paper No. 111 (Geneva, 1982), Preface p. x.

[22] Lukas Vischer, "The Process of Reception in the Ecumenical Movement," *Mid-Stream,* 23, no. 3 (July, 1984) 277.

This process is clearly indicated in the text of BEM, especially when it deals with the acute problems of radical disagreement between the churches. The results of the intense dialogues of the last six decades, and the experience of sharing in the life of the churches beyond confessional boundaries, are adequately expressed in the form of suggestions for further investigation and growth in agreement. The link between baptism and confirmation as chrismation, the dispute over baptism of children or adults, the disagreement about the real presence of Christ in the Eucharist, the episcopal and non-episcopal ministry, the sacerdotal and non-sacerdotal ministry, the individual and communal understanding of apostolic succession—all these problems are treated in a fresh way. This is the fruit of a deep and unshaken inner coherence which is deeply rooted in the consciousness of the transcending reality of the *one* tradition in the apostolic Church, a tradition which one has fully experienced as partners in an authentic ecumenical dialogue including faithfulness, loyalty and devotion both to one's own particular tradition and to the koinonia of the churches in the making.

By receiving in this sense, therefore, you are not forced to create "consensus" by betraying your own confessional status or abandoning your particular approach in matters of faith—thus relativizing it for the sake of a confessional syncretism. In reality you are invited to confirm the importance of belonging together with others who stand in the same apostolic tradition. However, this kind of "reception," which has to be distinguished from a simple "response," definitely signifies that one is willing and open to accept the fact that there are ways of approaching the truth and reality of faith other than one's own, and that it can be expressed in different ways. This, of course, is provided that there is no contradiction with the biblical and church tradition, no modifying of the essence and application of this truth in church life so that one no longer recognizes it as church faith and praxis. Certainly the demarcation line on this basic issue is not and cannot be clear; but one should not, on account of this difficulty, refrain from clearly defining the *limits* of openness to new concepts as we seek to advance in "consensus" by the method of convergence as is illustrated in BEM. Edward J. Kilmartin very appropriately remarks that "reception as an ecclesiological reality implies the formation of corporate openness which takes place through bearers of reception who may be juridical or non-juridical authorities. When a significant spiritual good is newly introduced into a global perception of the life of faith and thereby begins to affect the practice of the faith a new synthesis of understanding and practice of the faith is initiated."[23]

---

[23]Edward J. Kilmartin, *Journal of Ecumenical Studies,* 21 (1984) 37.

To exemplify this approach we could refer to the most disputed item of this convergence document, i.e., the section on Ministry. From the Orthodox point of view the old disagreements with the evangelical-Protestant attitude still persist; but one does not find in the text the same old-fashioned polemical phrases, and this allows us to discover new ways of meeting each other. Thus it is not absolutely clear in the text whether the personal, ministerial priesthood differs in nature from the general priesthood of all Christians, or whether priestly ordination is clearly a sacramental enacting and representing of the priesthood of Christ or just a sacramental act of *ministerial* ordination, which comes as an "order" directly from God. The question can be raised: for transmitting the apostolic tradition of the church and the fullness of the apostolic faith, does BEM consider the episcopal, sacerdotal ministry *together with* personal succession to be essential and absolutely necessary?

On the other hand, even given this difficult problematic persisting in BEM, its "openness" for converging elements (including adopting well-known Orthodox terminology) allows us to trace promising new approaches towards a better mutual understanding in the future. This is in *addition* to the already clear consensus achieved in many areas: the ordained ministry as essential for the church, for building the body of Christ, and for celebrating sacraments; the ministry of "episcopé" as needed in the Church, the ministry as it developed historically into a threefold pattern, etc. The distinction of the special ministry is approved, but not yet sufficiently defined; ministry is identified with presiding at the eucharist; it is appropriate to refer to ordained ministers as priests, because they fulfill a priestly service in imitation of Christ; episcopal succession is important for the Church to remain in the apostolic Tradition; ordination is sacramental in nature; invocation of the Spirit and laying on of hands is an important historical sign in the act of ordination and should be recovered by those churches that do not have it; ordination is unrepeatable; a genuine ministry of Christ and the charisms of the Spirit are present in the ministry of the major Christian churches today and are recognizable as such.[24]

The reference to the most difficult issue of BEM should convince the reader that there are indeed new dialectical approaches to key issues, and the aim of advancing towards new consensus. It is hardly surprising that the text does not immediately convince the Protestant-presbyterial church communities that episcopal ministry is absolutely

---

[24]I select these points from the list presented by Joseph F. Egan, S.J., in his article, "Ordained Ministry in BEM. A Theological Critique," *Mid-Stream,* 23, no. 3 (July, 1984) 290-91.

necessary for the Church; but BEM does urge the non-episcopal churches to "recover the sign of the episcopal succession."[25]

It is inevitable on this basis to speak of a "revitalization" of the understanding of ministry, following the general scheme and the spirit of the text as one of convergence and for the renewal of church life as a whole. BEM makes the point: "The truth of the Gospel could only be present through prophetic and charismatic leaders . . . reforms required a special ministry" (Ministry 33).

BEM does not give "partial positions" which are defended as pro-Catholic or pro-Protestant. Reading the text one can, of course, isolate phrases and judge the whole text on this basis. But this is an inappropriate way to read it and to understand the special meaning of "reception" which is signified and requested by it. As a matter of fact, one who recognizes the insistence of BEM on ordination as a kind of sacramental act, or on episcopal ministry, or on the threefold ministry as positive elements for the unity of the Church can arrive at the conclusion that the text betrays a philo-sacramental, philo-Catholic and especially philo-Orthodox attitude. Indeed many critical voices on the side of the Protestant world would agree with this.

As Orthodox we must admit that, as Joseph F. Egan, S.J. writes, "Non-episcopal churches could rightly object that far more is being asked of them than of episcopal churches."[26] He defends the thesis further that the Ministry text "is convinced that the best and perhaps only basis for mutual recognition of ministry and eventual union is precisely to recover the so-called Catholic values and practices of the early undivided Church."[27]

We should not seek here in the text a "partial position," but rather note the elements which *have been* recognized, by those whose lack of them in their church life is hindering them from contributing essentially to the maintenance of that unity of the Church which is given by the Spirit. Here what we called to "receive," as the result of the ecumenical fellowship and dialogues, is an invitation to self-criticism with regard to elements which are lacking, or distorted, or others which are exaggerated in the cause of "unity and renewal." The request of BEM for "reception" is an appeal to all of the churches to examine themselves in the light of the urgent need for reunion and renewal. One must become critical of one's own stances to ask whether they are, by their one-sided, non-dialogical attitudes, unnecessary hindrances on the road

---

[25]See *Baptism, Eucharist and Ministry,* Faith and Order Paper No. 111 (Geneva, 1982), Ministry 53.

[26]Joseph F. Egan, "Ordained Ministry," p. 297.

[27]Ibid., p. 301.

to unity. Father J. Egan again gives us an example by questioning his own Roman Catholic tradition which, of course, must have a serious objection against BEM since there is no reference to the so-called "Petrine Ministry." Indeed, without this there can be no full debate on Ministry for this tradition. Egan says that "were the Roman Catholic Church to fail to act on the consensus achieved in the bilateral dialogues and the issues raised in BEM and particularly in the Ministry text, she might find herself in the unenviable position of blocking further progress towards unity at the very time the Reformation churches are showing strong desire for unity and a willingness to move closer to the Catholic Church and thus unwittingly letting the *kairos* of this stage of the ecumenical moment pass by. It is no secret that, as Pope Paul VI so candidly said: 'The Pope, as we well know, is undoubtedly the gravest obstacle in the path of ecumenism,' so there are those today who consider the Roman Catholic Church a major obstacle to meaningful progress towards church unity despite its truly great contribution through the theological dialogues."[28]

This kind of self-judgment, while one remains faithful to one's own church tradition, is inherent in the process of reception of BEM within the experience of the ecumenical dialogues. Of course some theologians in all of the churches will oppose "reception" in this self-critical sense of opening themselves to new ecumenical perspectives. This may be because of their strict adherence to the *grammata* of their confessional statements or juridical canonical structures and laws, or because they have not been exposed to ecumenical fellowship, dialogue or mutual spiritual edification with other Christians outside their own tradition. They will accuse BEM of being syncretistic or radically pro-Protestant, or (which is most usual today) unduly pro-Catholicizing and philo-Orthodox.

This criticism cuts across all present denominational barriers, creating a trans-confessional reactionary group motivated by completely different or even opposed theological premises, from extreme free-church Protestantism to the most rigid Orthodoxy, but all marked by the same anti-ecumenical zeal. This is either because they have been deprived of authentic ecumenical dialogues, or they have misunderstood them as betraying church tradition by attempting an amalgamation of doctrines for the sake of illegitimate "consensus." They will consequently urge their church authorities either to repudiate BEM, or to respond and comment only for the sake of defending a particular position. This may be defending the rights of the Reformation and saving it from an eventual absorption within sacramental Catholicism; or

---

[28]Ibid., p. 304.

safeguarding the uniqueness of Roman Catholicism and saving it from revolutionary Protestant elements which would disrupt the solid, inner disposition of the Roman Catholic Church; or, finally, preserving unchanged the holy ancient tradition of Orthodoxy and saving it from the "ecumenist's betrayal" which surrenders the purity and accuracy of the Orthodox faith, turning it into a weak liberal stance to accomodate "modernism."

At the same time, however, there is another trans-confessional group which is growing along with texts like BEM. This group is composed of those who share in the results of ecumenical dialogues, learning to respect more seriously their own tradition, but also listening to the voices of others who are partners in the common struggle for unity, for which each works by renewing the life of their own church. They are looking forward to a continuous and progressive development of genuine efforts towards building a worldwide conciliar fellowship of the one Church, based on Word, Tradition and Sacrament and centered on the Eucharist and the kerygma, in diakonia to the world and its renewal. This Orthodox-evangelical-catholicity will keep urging all church authorities of all confessional families not only to respond and comment on, but also to "receive," BEM as a process of growth in the one apostolic Church through honest self-examination and self-judgment.

4. Orthodoxy facing the reception of BEM

The Orthodox Church in particular has to "receive" BEM as the fruit of ecumenical dialogues up to this point, dialogues in which she has actively participated right from the beginning. The Lima document makes manifest, more than ever before, the positive Orthodox contribution in the realm of ecclesiology. The Orthodox involvement in the Commission of Faith and Order goes right back to 1927. In BEM, the trinitarian theology with its emphasis on pneumatology and charismatic approach to sacramental theology centered around the eucharist as the sacrament of the Church *par excellence,* a respect for apostolic tradition as it has been handed down throughout the centuries to the Church, an eschatological faith in the Risen Lord as the head of the Body—all these are evident signs of the central role that the Orthodox have played in the ecumenical dialogues within the fellowship of the churches. It would be a great pity if the majority of the Orthodox Churches decide to abdicate at this crucial moment and only respond from "a distance," criticizing, on the basis of a one-sided scholastic dogmatic and comparative theology, what they have achieved as active and responsible partners with theologians of other churches, who have carefully listened to the Orthodox voice and given to the Orthodox contribution its appropriate prominent place.

We have to admit that, more than other church communities, the Orthodox ones suffer from a discouraging *ambivalent* ecumenical attitude. The ecumenical movement to a great extent remains for them still a rather foreign and imported "Protestant" ideology, and the "ecumenist" appears somehow to be a strange figure. The ecumenical dialogues, and even more the ecumenical fellowship, are restricted within hierarchical structures affecting only a small circle of specialists, or specially interested people, who have no access to the great masses of the Orthodox, especially in the ancient Orthodox mother Churches of the East. Under these circumstances it is certain that for most of the Orthodox Churches BEM cannot be authentically "received" in the manner described above, and that there will be no effective process of "reception" as described by the four questions of the Preface to BEM.

In this respect the situation is almost hopeless. This is because our Churches have not been really exposed to ecumenism and are not employing the appropriate channels. Furthermore, in most cases the Churches are not open to ecumenical developments and are deprived of the ecumenical ethos necessary to "receive" such a document, and to act accordingly, as consistent members of the ecumenical fellowship, allowing it to persuade the hearts and minds both of the lay faithful and of the whole of the priesthood in the parishes.[29]

Representing the correct Orthodox approach in this respect, Alekos Papaderos, the Director of the Orthodox Academy in Crete, Greece, writes: "Even if such a universal consensus were to be achieved at the highest level of authority competent here, it would have a real chance only if it were to fill the heart and conscience of the shepherds and the faithful with the assurance that doctrinal differences of a kind which were fundamental and strong enough to separate us from the love of Christ and from communion with him and with one another no longer existed. The only way to prepare a consensus of this kind and to make the way for such an assurance is for synods, church authorities, congregations, theological colleges, church mass media, our Christian education and our daily dealings with human beings who differ from us in faith and in thought to be filled and directed by the Spirit and by the style and breadth of approach of the Lima text, i.e., by the eucharistic experience of God, of the fellow human being, and of the world."[30]

---

[29]See for this issue the excellent article by Alekos Papaderos: "Some Thoughts on Reception: Not Forgetting the People and Life," especially the section: "A Reception Which Does Not Bypass the Pleroma of the Church," *Mid-Stream,* 23, no. 1 (January, 1984) 50-63.

[30]Ibid., p. 63.

These correct suggestions express fully the authentic Orthodox spirit or ethos, and the tradition which fights for truth in love and loves others in truth, not imprisoning itself in the *gramma* which kills the spirit, all the while being based on sound and unshaken Orthodox principles identical with those of the one undivided, holy, catholic and apostolic Church. Unfortunately these suggestions appear for many Orthodox leaders wishful thinking and a utopia, if not a heretical approach of some "ecumenists." For Father Thomas Hopko, the Orthodox are "overwhelmingly positive to BEM because they find the statement both in spirit and content to be simply a very good one, and Orthodox commentators generally believe what is said, and find the way it is said to be basically sacred and right and . . . the document presents a view of baptism, eucharist and ministry with which the Orthodox can for the most part heartily agree." But I am afraid that Father Hopko is expressing the real situation when he writes: "The greatest anxiety found among Orthodox commentators of the Lima text is that some churches will not treat it at all seriously, because they consider the issues with which it deals to be secondary and unimportant . . . and will prove themselves to be unable to respond to BEM as churches and others which may do so merely in a formal manner, but also that others may treat the whole effort with indifference, cynicism or outright contempt."[31]

This remark refers to recipient churches in general, but I am afraid that it may be valid for the majority of the Orthodox ones, and especially their authorities at this moment. This would not only be the result of their ignorance of, or indifference towards, ecumenical dialogues but comes also from a kind of introverted theology carried out by theologians who, because of their defensive non-Orthodox scholastic conservatism, become the only spokesmen of their Churches and have access to both church leadership structures and to church people, and affect both of these categories negatively on the delicate matter of ecumenical dialogue.

There is, on the one hand, a reformed liberalism, expressed by well-known theologians as individuals, not in agreement with the consciousness of their church. This results in a kind of anti-sacramental attitude, and therefore to a cynical stance towards BEM, because "it says so many and big words and things in praising sacraments, that one may think and understand that the fullness, validity and glory of the work of Christ needs the assistance of clergy in order to become effective. . . . " And further, referring to the use of the biblical verse "Great is the mystery of faith" (1 Tim 3.16) by BEM and the Lima

---

[31]Thomas Hopko, "The Lima Statement and the Orthodox," *The Search for Visible Unity,* ed. Jeffrey Gros (New York, 1984), pp. 55 and 57.

Liturgy (para 22), there is the comment: "It is less to Christ that this refers than to the miraculous change of bread and wine" and that the treatment of Ministry "points in a direction which does not exclude a claim of monopoly."[32]

There is, on the other hand, a false Orthodox conservatism which arrives at the same stance regarding the reception of BEM. This generalizes on the basis of an abstract notion of "Protestantism" using individual, reformed liberalism as the only criterion of "Protestant" faith and lumping all churches of the Reformation into one anti-sacramental confession—as if this represented the entire body of churches which stand over against the Orthodox as partners in the ecumenical movement.

It is not extraordinary that such an Orthodox theologian cannot advise his Church to "receive" the document. His criticism uses the ecclesiological issue to disqualify all of the non-Orthodox churches as non-churches, and all of their sacraments as having no status of ecclesial meaning and validity whatsoever, finding the use of the term "church" in BEM "irritating" and finally remarking for all of them together that "without sacerdotal ministry and apostolic succession there is no Church and consequently there is no holy Eucharist."[33] It is evident that, on this base, the "ecumenical" suggestion to the Orthodox Church authorities regarding BEM's reception is simply "not to reject it," because it is "useful for the tragically-divided Protestant world" (and what has the Orthodox rejection or acceptance to do with the use or rejection of the text by the Protestants?). This attitude forgets that the text has been produced and endorsed unanimously by Roman Catholics and Orthodox and Anglican Church representatives, following the comments of their official church bodies, which are not in union and communion amongst themselves even though they do have sacraments, sacramental sacerdotal episcopé, and apostolic succession fully recognized between the first two, and partly recognized between them and the third church communion.

Certainly in both of these cases one cannot expect or even speak of "reception" of BEM as the result of ecumenical dialogues and current common ecumenical church life, work, prayer, and mission. It is a great pity that these two examples are followed by many church leaders and theologians who have ecumenical experience, but are deprived of

---

[32]Markus Barth, "Fragen und Erwagungen zu den Lima-Papieren," *Kirchenblatt fur die reformierte Schweiz*, No. 20 (1984), p. 324.

[33]See G. Konidaris, "The Catholic Orthodox Facing the Three Texts of the World Council of Churches and of the Proposal of Lima," *Symposium for Archbishop Seraphim*, p. 333 (in Greek).

a right evangelical or genuine Orthodox ecumenical vision. It is astonishing how these two extremes of radical liberalism and false conservatism meet together and "exploit" each other as they face the complicated affair of receiving a text like BEM resulting from present-day ecumenical dialogue. They help each other in caricaturing the use of the term "church" by BEM, and the ecumenical movement as a whole as well as its sacramental approach. For the one extreme position, the use of the term is due to an abuse of the sacrament; for the other, a false application of it. In both cases the text becomes non-receivable and, of course, "dangerous" for church life and theology. It is too "liberal" (as non-sacramental) for a rigid Orthodox-conservative, and it is too clerical-sacramentalistic for a radical Reformed. Such strangely similar attitudes can certainly not be satisfied by BEM. They are, however, bypassed by this same text of BEM, and transcended by a new attitude which invites the churches to a self-affirmation through their readiness to remain open to a new perspective in interpreting church divisions, evaluating them in new ways suggested by this text in order gradually and carefully to overcome them.

5. Reception and self-affirmation in Orthodoxy

Reflecting, therefore, on the Orthodox Churches in connection with the reception of BEM one has to suggest respectfully to them that, along with the expression of their dogmatic position they should also reflect self-critically upon their own life. It is appropriately observed by an Orthodox theologian: "How can the Orthodox demand from others for the sake of recognition what it does not demand from its own members, not only in practice but also in theory"[34] (with a view to Eucharist being the center of church life without however implying frequent communion, infant baptism without a firm community life and the parents' faith, the incorrect application of functions of church authorities without lay participation, lack of collegiality within the one Priesthood, etc.)? Here one does not oppose Orthodoxy to orthopraxy, thus shifting the ecclesiological issue to ethical categories. Rather one refers to the self-identity of the Orthodox on the crucial matters of ecclesiology. This must be examined as the Orthodox exclude other churches from having the ecclesial nature and character which they profess, and from the ecumenical fellowship—that is, disqualifying the essence and life of their church as well as their mission, evangelism and devotion, their very identity as churches! This is to refuse to acknowledge their generations of believers in the past, as well as their present dynamic presence in today's world.

---

[34]Thomas Hopko, "The Lima Statement," p. 61.

It would have been, in other words, a fatal mistake and self-denial on the part of the Orthodox if they had rejected BEM, or repudiated it theologically by criticizing it in a radical destructive way, precisely at the moment when there are such critical voices on the side of radical reformed theologians, because for them the text reveals a strong catholicizing ecclesiology. Friedrich Beisser raises the question "whether (in BEM) space is left for evangelical Christendom . . . " urging "Protestant theology to see the dangers of an uncritical coincidence of God and Church."[35] Eilert Herms also shows "where the Lima text on ordained ministry contradicts the Lutheran tradition. . . . the center of the conflict is the Lima doctrine of ordination as sacrament which is wholly unacceptable from a Lutheran point of view."[36] P. Buhler, finally, remarks in the same direction : "On the sacrament and the ministries the text is characterized by its very great concern to respect tradition. It envisages reestablishing a clericalism which is rather anachronistic in view of the modern situation."[37]

We Orthodox must reflect very carefully, reasoning theologically in a spirit of self-criticism, receiving, answering and commenting upon BEM. And in the way in which we respond to BEM we face the risk of betraying ourselves. The manner through which we shall, or shall not receive BEM, in the light of past and current ecumenical dialogues, will demonstrate where we stand as Orthodox, i.e., how consistent and serious we are about Orthodoxy being the *center* of the ecumenical movement and one of its main founders as the church of and for unity *par excellence.* In particular we will show whether we are able to discern the times and grasp our own existence as the Church catholic and apostolic in unbroken continuity, authentically rooted in her life and thought. The "reception" of BEM will be for all churches, but especially for the Orthodox, the testing ground of their own self-identity. Do we really want church reunion? Are we ready to deny our self-sufficiency and accept the risk to change what has conditioned and limited Orthodox openness and the ecumenicity of our patristic theology? Are we ready to incorporate in our thought and actions anything concrete that has occurred, any event or experience in our life as a person and as Church, during these last sixty years of ecumenical participation and dialogue?

Nicolas Lossky, dealing as an Orthodox with the Lima text in this way and trying to answer its challenge for a self-critical approach on

---

[35]Thesen zur Konvergenzerklärung über "Taufe, Eucharistie, Amt," *Kerygma und Dogma,* (1985/1), p. 32.

[36]"Stellungnahme zum dritten Teil des Lima-Dokumentes. Amt," ibid., p. 96.

[37]"Un point de vue critique," *Etudes Théologiques et Religieuses,* 1984, p. 530.

the part of the churches when receiving it, raises the question: "To which *metanoia* is the Lima text inviting the Orthodox Church?" He remarks: "This text, as does the whole of the ecumenical movement, strongly reminds the Orthodox Church of her vocation to permanent conversion to Orthodoxy, understood as the fulness of life in Christ. The *metanoia* is not a momentary act but a 'turning' which implies a permanent attitude of being impelled toward union by the submission of the human will to the divine will."[38]

In receiving BEM, we reconfirm our own ecumenicity in theory and praxis in a consistent way in accepting that ecumenicity concerns the authenticity of Orthodoxy, that the unity of the church is our primary concern, and that Orthodox renewal today depends also upon our active sharing in ecumenical work and dialogue. Reception is a long process of church life in reconstruction together with the other church communities, and not simply a "yes" or "no" statement by institutional authorities. It is only in the consistent praxis of the churches acting together as one spiritual community in today's world that this kind of reception is going to be realized. After such long and comprehensive theological work done within the Faith and Order Commission and the ecumenical dialogue as a whole, our praxis is surely the proof of the authenticity of our ecumenicity. Jürgen Moltmann makes the right remark: "At the present time, ecumenical theology seems to be and to have developed to a point from which it can make no further headway unless there are changes in the churches' praxis."[39]

Certainly BEM is not a perfect document and we must guard ourselves from all kinds of ecumenical triumphalism. It has many deficiencies and for the Orthodox it is subject to criticism in several of its theses, concerning for example the link between baptism and confirmation, the exact reference to the real presence of Christ in the elements of the eucharist, the full description of the sacerdotal episcopal ministry and the unreserved affirmation of the "personal" apostolic succession. All Orthodox who have accepted and appreciated it have clearly shown this by their critical but at the same time appreciative remarks. This is evident because BEM is not an Orthodox, Protestant or Catholic confession.

There are already such constructive Orthodox criticisms which appreciate the positive contribution of the Lima text as a genuine effort towards reunion. This criticism indicates that the Orthodox Churches can be appreciative of the convergence achieved by BEM. They can,

---

[38]Nicholas Lossky, "A quelle 'metanoia' le texte de Lima appellet-il l'Eglise Orthodoxe?" *Unité des Chrétiens,* No. 57, 1985, p. 23.

[39]*What Kind of Unity?* Faith and Order Paper No. 82 (Geneva, 1977), p. 39.

therefore, respond to it positively even while expressing their critical comments and envisaging a long process of "reception" in the future. We find an example of such constructive criticism in the special issue of *St. Vladimir's Theological Quarterly,* Vol. 27, No. 4, 1983. In the editorial we read: "The Orthodox impact upon the document is universally seen as very substantial, if not decisive."[40] It refers to the frequent complaint that the Orthodox participation in ecumenical debates is often reduced to useless attempts at influencing the Protestant majority" and the editorial adds: "This time the influence is there; the document contains a sacramental understanding of the Church, respect for and reference to the faith of the Church throughout the ages, a definition of the episcopate as normative for the apostolic ministry, etc."[41]

In this critical-appreciative attitude the reader encounters a series of positive statements like: "That many non-episcopal, less traditional, and less sacramental Christian churches seem prepared to approve much of the Lima statement appears to many from the Orthodox and Catholic tradition to be nothing short of a sensational ecumenical advance."[42] Regarding the section on the Eucharist we read further the observation of Vladimir Berzonsky: "So much of the work represents solid Orthodox doctrine and practice, reflecting . . . input from those with such classical liturgical perspectives."[43] George Bebis adds, "The document is of an ecumenical nature and tries hard to achieve a common understanding, a common thinking and feeling on this sacrament of sacraments; in that connection the Lima statement is a great contribution toward a common bond of love and understanding and rapprochement."[44] Alkiviadis Calivas, in dealing with the section on Baptism, makes several critical remarks—the document is fond of using "sign" for "sacrament" or "mystery," the defeat of Satan is not clearly stated in Baptism, the question of infant baptism in connection with chrismation, etc. But as an Orthodox he praises the document because "despite its several deficiencies, it presents some exciting possibilities for an interesting dialogue both for those who share a more common belief and for those who may disagree or be further apart on one or more issues. . . . The Orthodox can adopt its outline while adapting its content, to present the essential teachings of the Church on the mysteries of baptism and chrismation. It is also an effective tool for

---

[40]See St. Vladimir's Theological Quarterly, 27, No. 4, 237.

[41]Ibid., 223.

[42]James Jorgenson, "Reflections on the Lima Statement," ibid., p. 249.

[43]"BEM, A Pastor's View," ibid., 253.

[44]"The Lima Statement on the Eucharist," ibid., 271.

exposing mature Orthodox Christians to the views of others."[45]
Finally, Robert Stephanopulos in examining the section on the Ministry
writes: "The statement goes far beyond the previous method of comparative ecclesiology, placing the issue of ministry in a total trinitarian,
ecclesiological and sacramental setting. This certainly supports the Orthodox insistence on a proper theological, ecclesiological and eucharistic
approach to the issue of ministries, as well as to the often misunderstood
Orthodox firmness against inter-communion as a means rather than
the end of visible unity. . . . " Further he remarks that "the ministry
(for the BEM text) of the *episcopé* in particular is necessary to express
and safeguard the unity of the body. This is not an unqualified endorsement of the threefold pattern of ministry, to be sure. Nevertheless, it
provides a strong affirmation of the practice of the early Church as
understood by the Orthodox and gives strong endorsement to the resolution of this aspect of the recognition of ministries against the polemical
background of the Middle Ages. Thus papalism, presbyterianism and
congregationalism as extreme positions are rejected as visible options
of church order in a mutually recognized ministry."[46]

Such a critical appreciation of the document illustrates the ethos
of "reception" of the BEM text. Such "reception" will express Orthodox ecclesial consciousness and Orthodox theology while bearing
in mind that this document, representing the results of the ecumenical
dialogues, does not pretend to be a new credal form and, therefore,
does not expect "reception" in its traditional canonical meaning. Rather
it is offered to the churches as reflecting their *own* converging trends
in doctrine as a result of their ecumenical dialogical relationship and
as an instrument toward their future consensus.

An example also in this respect can be found in the common declaration of the Orthodox and Roman Catholic Consultative Group in the
United States of America, presided over by Metropolitan Silas and
Bishop A. O'Neill and published in *Episkepsis,* No. 326, January 1985,
pp. 11-16. Further, a remarkable constructive response can be found
in the critical-appreciative remarks of the Faith and Order Advisory
Group of the Anglican Church. After a long, systematic and detailed
critical survey of the BEM text (very instructive also for the Orthodox!)
one can read in the conclusions: "We recognize in the Lima text . . .
the faith of the Church through the ages. The group is thankful for
the remarkable theological convergence registered in all three texts and
believes that it will be possible . . . to move further towards that consensus necessary to support the visible unity of the Church in one faith

---

[45]"The Lima Statement on Baptism," ibid., 261.
[46]"The Lima Statement on Ministry," ibid., 277.

and one eucharistic fellowship expressed in worship and common life in Christ, in order that the world might believe.''[47]

6. "Reception" as a pointer to future ecumenical growth on the basis of "ecclesiality"

To clarify further the issue of "reception" of BEM it is helpful to define other terms which are closely related to "reception." The well-known Roman Catholic theologian Yves Congar helps us in this respect by suggesting the following distinctions: *"Convergence:* this is more a matter of a dynamism towards a goal than of a substantial agreement. *Agreed statement:* agreement on a particular point, leaving more or less profound differences in others. *Consensus or Full Agreement:* a total agreement at least in context, if not in expression. *Substantial Agreement:* this relates to a basic nucleus without which the message of salvation is not transmitted in its integrity, while accepting that neither doctrinal elaboration nor practice correspond among the partner churches. The essentials are assured and there is the same shared intention of faith.''[48]

Using these terms one could say that "reception" in the case of BEM is meant in the direction and spirit of the last definition, i.e., "substantial agreement," and that it presupposes both "convergence" and "agreed statements" and envisages, for the future, a continuing growth towards "consensus" or "full agreement." When, therefore, the churches are invited to "receive" this text, it is not demanded that they endorse it either as a confession of faith or as a consensus statement of full agreement. (The Preface of BEM clearly indicates that it is not yet a "consensus," thus helping us to avoid a misunderstanding.) The churches are, rather, respectfully asked to accept BEM as representing a nucleus of substantial agreement on the fundamental essentials of the apostolic faith, and to recognize that it will be fruitful for the churches' further progress towards reaching church reunion in the future.

An unwritten presupposition definitely lies behind the Lima text. This is the idea that, while accepting the concept of the limits of the Church, following its confessional identity or clear canonical definitions, one recognizes that there is a kind of "ecclesiality" that churches do share in their ecumenical fellowship, on the basis of essential elements of the biblical notion of *Ecclesia.*

These elements are the common belief of all of the churches that

---

[47] *Towards a Church of England Response to BEM and ARCIC* (London, 1985), p 103.

[48] Yves Congar, "Diversity and Communion," SCM Press 1984, p. 140, quoted in *Towards a Church of England Response to BEM and ARCIC,* p. 8.

there is but one catholic and apostolic Church, and that we must remain rooted in this one church while seeking visible organic unity, understood and practiced in full union and communion; that this Church, throughout the centuries, has been marked by the one apostolic creed embodied in the Nicene-Constantinopolitan formula; that as basic and indispensable sacraments for salvation we must accept baptism in the name of the Holy Trinity (including confirmation) and the eucharist; that the eucharist must be administered by a specially ordained ministry in communal and personal unbroken succession from the Apostles, as keeping and manifesting the historic unbroken continuity of the Church (even if this is not, for the moment, accepted on the basis of episcopal, sacerdotal priestly identity as it should be according to the Orthodox catholic faith); and, finally, the life of the Church as it is expressed by church communities in evangelism, witness, mission and diakonia in the world in the name of Christ and by the invocation of the Spirit. This kind of "ecclesiality" seems to me an essential presupposition for understanding the basis of ecumenical dialogues and their converging reports, and, in particular the text of BEM and the type of "reception" that the WCC is asking from the churches. For a more elaborated exposition of the notion of "ecclesiality" see my essay: "Die Zugehörigkeit zur Kirche nach orthodoxische Verständnis."[49]

Certainly the ecumenical situation is in many respects discouraging and does not allow for any easy optimism. I know very well how difficult it is for an Orthodox to experience theological and ecumenical fellowship with the principle of the Church as *"semper reformanda"* when this is represented by radical reformed theologians and some Protestant church communities which are centered exclusively on the principle of the Word of God, understood in a unilateral sense as opposing church tradition as a joint criterion of apostolic faith along with the biblical heritage. Certainly a great part of Protestantism seems, in the Orthodox perspective—and rightly so—to be centrifugal, always adopting new stances which are further away from the center, while the Orthodox believe that they are approaching the center. Certainly much of Protestantism is always insisting, in an intense way, of new practices in the church (such as the ordination of women), thus rendering agreement more difficult for the Orthodox. But, as Orthodox, we must always remember that this is not the *whole* of the ecumenical movement, and that of course this attitude does not represent the whole of Protestantism dominating the whole of ecumenical dialogue, as some

---

[49]"Die Zugehörigkeit zur Kirche nach orthodoxische Verständnis," in the symposium edited by P. Meinhold, *Das Problem der Kirchengliedschaft heute* (Wissenschaftliche Buchgesellschaft, 1979), pp. 366-91.

Orthodox, in their criticism of the WCC and their total rejection of the usefulness of the ecumenical dialogues seem to believe. Certainly as Orthodox we find problems in other churches. These are due either to facile generalizations, or because of a basic element which is missing in other churches, or because there is a false application in the realm of ministry (i.e., the papal application of the Petrine ministry). BEM, in reality, is inviting the churches to go deeper together into the substance of the apostolic faith and its experience in the life of the Church throughout the ages. A Roman Catholic theologian, John Coventry, S.J., shows how to grasp this deeper reference of BEM in such delicate matters. The Lima text, when dealing with the ministry, avoids speaking of "orders," preferring to speak of "charisma." This is, of course, closer to the Eastern than to the Western Church tradition. Referring to this, he makes the constructive remark: "And if orderly transmission of powers is no longer considered essential for the validity of a ministry, the way would appear to be open for recognition of and cooperation with Western ministries. The role of the papacy would then be seen prmarily in terms of responsibility for the unity of the Church."[50]

In addition we must be aware that inter-church relationships are also underdeveloped and inspire no optimism because of the frequent absence of a proper ecumenical zeal and action on the part of ecclesiastical authorities and constituencies. Thus BEM "descends upon" a variety of frustrated and frustrating church bodies and theological circles which lack appropriate ecumenical experience and appreciation of what "reception" could mean today in light of such a document. The former Director of the Faith and Order Commission, Professor W. Lazareth, faces this discrepancy with his humorous remark: "Canonically to receive is the highest form of church reaction, while parliamentarily to receive is precisely the lowest. This is our challenge and opportunity: the eager doctrinal hens have come home to roost among very nervous and inexperienced juridical roosters, and no one is quite sure just how much egg is going to end up in whose face."

Thus BEM, received not as an isolated text but one which incorporates the results of ecumenical dialogues, signifies a breakthrough of particular importance for the ecumenical movement in the area of ecclesiology from an ecumenical perspective. The beginning has been made, regardless of difficult ecumenical relations and of some frustrating local church situations, where the ecumenical task is faced with hesitation and reluctance. It is a text for realization in the long-

---

[50]John Coventry, S.J., "The Lima Report: Responses to Baptism, Eucharist and Ministry," *One in Christ,* (1984/1), p. 7.

term future. It is a hopeful sign now for a long process of regathering, through new perspectives on ecclesiology, the separated churches. In spite of its deficiencies as they appear only too plainly to the critical reader today, the coming generations will cherish its effects gladly.

This must be our hope in order to continue our work with persever-ance, defeating pessimism and the attitudes of ecumenical indifference. We will be encouraged by the preliminary stage of consensus already achieved, and above all by invoking the Spirit of God who is the Spirit of reception insofar as he is the Spirit of newness and renewal in the Church and the world. If we are really honest and right in our efforts, the Paraclete, the Spirit of truth will forward, strengthen and perfect this kind of dynamic "reception" in the churches from now on into the future.

We may finally conclude that "reception" is proposed to the churches by the constitution of the WCC because the BEM document is regarded by them as the result of its fellowship of churches and of the ecumenical dialogues of the last six decades. It included in its draft-ing process the maximum ecumenical representation possible today, transcending even its own membership. "Reception" means that the churches can recognize in this text the fullest statement possible today of their common action on crucial issues now separating them in the realm of ecclesiology, together with the intention to bridge their dif-ferences in the future. "Reception" in the light of BEM signifies for the churches that its text can convince people of good will in all of the churches who aspire for unity as the heart of the Gospel message, and that all of our differences are yet rooted in the unshaken biblical and apostolic elements of the one tradition of the Christian Church com-munity in all ages. "Reception" is respectfully suggested to the churches because BEM can become for them, if they are ready to use it for pro-moting Christian unity as their common witness in today's world, a pre-consensus document consisting of promising converging elements of faith of particular importance today, thus allowing all churches to look ahead together with hopeful expectations.

Response to Nikos Nissiotis: "The Meaning of Reception in Relation to the Results of Ecumenical Dialogue on the Basis of Faith and Order Document 'Baptism, Eucharist and Ministry' "

BISHOP NERSES BOZABALIAN

OUR CATHOLICATE AND BISHOPS have received with great appreciation the BEM document. We realize the great importance and value of the step taken in BEM by the fellowship of churches in the ecumenical movement in the WCC on the road to the eventual realization of the visible unity for which we all aspire in order to manifest our oneness in the Lord Jesus Christ and to witness for the glory of his kingdom.

This initial consensus, which is the gift of the Holy Spirit to the universal Church in our time, fills us with hope for solid progress in the coming decades. It gives us courage to go forward together for making our mission effective in bringing the Gospel to our people.

Our Church has been engaged in the ecumenical endeavor of the Faith and Order Commission to the extent of its ability in the difficult circumstances in which it has found itself in the course of the decades since the beginning of the emergence of the ecumenical movement of this century.

In receiving BEM we feel our bond with other churches in the ecumenical fellowship strengthened. Of course, much greater work still lies ahead to be done, particularly in the field of ecclesiology, which appears to be the crucial problem to be taken up for an eventual solution.

Our conversations with the Eastern Orthodox and with the Roman Catholics (Vienna 1968, 1971, 1973, 1978, and in the United States) have brought forth the fact that our separations are not of depth and substance, but rather of a terminological nature, accentuated by political, social and cultural adverse factors.

75

However, we are grateful for the success achieved in the production of BEM, which makes us feel closer to traditions and confessions other than ours in the apostolic faith and makes us realize more vividly our fundamental unity with them in orthodoxy and orthopraxy.

Our estrangement with other ancient church traditions of East and West goes further back than the eleventh century. Yet we are deeply gratified in finding, in the course of our modest involvement in the ecumenical movement, that the gap between us has been rather more like cracks on the surface than on the bedrock of the Orthodoxy of the wholeness of the conscious Church universal.

BEM, in a way, reinforces our consciousness of the reality; we receive BEM in this spirit.

It is our expectation that in continuing the work with BEM, the Faith and Order Commission will strive to clarify our vision of the nature of the unity we should seek, a unity which will operate as an effective council of churches that will give guidance on matters concerning the whole of Christendom in the proclamation of the Gospel of Christ. That is, a council of churches in communion with one another, a conciliar fellowship which will be neither a legislative body nor an executive body, but rather an evangelizing body giving guidance with a unified voice to churches and their peoples in the proclamation of the Gospel of Christ for the salvation of mankind. We receive BEM as a stepping-stone in the direction of such a goal and hope that BEM consensus will gradually, if slowly, permeate the thinking and attitude of teachers and preachers of all the member churches of the World Council.

The reception of BEM will inform us in our relationships, conciliar fellowships and cooperation with other churches. We find BEM in general in harmony with the apostolic faith. Therefore, we shall include BEM in our instructional literature for consideration.

BEM will be an important instrument in our common witness for the apostolic faith within the environment of the secular society where we find the Church.

BEM reinforces our consciousness of the fact that our estrangement and division of long centuries has not produced any fissure of significance in our common apostolic faith in the Church universal. BEM makes us discover the superficiality of our divisions which have been of a political, social and cultural nature.

BEM, in the method of its preparation and production, should and, we believe, will, be a model to follow in the bilateral and multilateral consultations and dialogues between churches, with a view to making them more productive in giving impetus to the work of unity.

In many instances when we put our differences in their proper context they appear in reality not divisive but rather as only different facets of the experiences of different traditions in their peculiar local life situations.

BEM shows us where we now stand in our common understanding of the fundamentals in certain areas of the faith in common with one another.

BEM is also very important in indicating the stepping-stones for further progress in convergence, for, in a sense, it maps out for us the direction to be taken on our dialogues with one another.

BEM is certainly not an additional credal formula to be attached to the ancient statements of faith, nor a new step forward from them. But rather a new initial meeting ground between differing church traditions, from which to start afresh our march towards the unity which we have been seeking in the past with more or less zeal and persistence, in order to respond to the call of the Lord Jesus, impelled by the Holy Spirit.

Unity is not a static concept embedded in formulas, but rather a dynamic conciliar fellowship in the pursuit of common goals for the promotion of the kingdom of God in Christ informed by the Holy Spirit. The reception of BEM will be such an act of fellowship in mind and spirit.

It is unrealistic and even hypocritical to think that the unity mandated by the Lord Jesus can or will be achieved by the conversion of the constituencies of one tradition to the other. Unity can be envisaged only as a progressive convergence of points in christology and ecclesiology on which we do and can stand together as churches.

We are inclined to think that in view of the involvement of the laity in the apostolate of the Church and the necessity of the active participation of lay persons in the upbuilding of the social and corporate life of the faithful in the Church, it is healthier to speak of the charismatic nature of the ministerial order rather than speak of its authoritarian aspect.

We have read carefully the study of Dr. Nissiotis with deep appreciation. His comprehensive analysis of the nature of "reception" in the modern ecumenical situation, to which BEM is addressed, appears to us thorough and persuasive. We hope that in the light of this study and in the sense in which reception is understood and described in it, BEM will be received generally and it will be, as a "pre-consensus document" and an effective instrument for the promotion of the work of the Faith and Order Commission in its pursuit of the visible unity of the churches in the future according to the Lord's will.

The Significance and Status of BEM in the Ecumenical Movement

ARCHBISHOP KIRILL

SEVENTY—FIVE YEARS have passed since the Edinburg Conference and sixty-five since the Geneva Preparatory Conference where the Orthodox participation in the ecumenical movement was started, but one may still hear an opinion that ecumenism belongs to the sphere of external church relations. The Lima document is particularly significant because it leaves no doubts about the interconnection between ecumenical relations among churches and their inner life. The clearer the churches comprehend this intrinsic meaning of ecumenism, the less ecumenism will resemble ''foreign policy of the churches'' and the more it will be inspired by theological, pastoral and missionary preconditions as well as by those of diakonia dictated by real needs of the churches which perform their ministry in the modern world.

These preliminary remarks give us ground to speak about the significance and status of BEM for the ecumenical movement and for the Orthodox Churches, for their inner life. The latter is the reason for analyzing the Lima document. This analysis does not claim to be complete and is not an official response of my Church.

1. Almost eight years separate Accra (1974) from Lima (1982) and they bear witness to quite successful activities of the Faith and Order Commission and—what is more important—to the growing ability of churches to carry on multilateral theological dialogue. As a result of the immense work done in this period of time the second version of the agreed theological document on Baptism, Eucharist and Ministry appeared. Undoubtedly, this document, in comparison with the previous one, is a substantial step forward along the way to the common expression of the apostolic Tradition and the faith of the early undivided Church. The Lima document shows the higher level of agreement

reached by a group which consisted of over one hundred theologians who represented practically all major confessions and the most important trends in contemporary Christian theology. This growth of consent confirms the right direction taken by the Faith and Order Commission in its work which is aimed at the achievement of theological agreements on the most important questions of Christian faith as well as the effectiveness of the chosen method.[1]

2. The Lima document has a well-defined and well-thought-out structure. The main text contains the agreed material, while the questions on which convergence has not been achieved are italicized in the form of commentaries. The tone and manner of exposition are positive. There are no imposed averments, nor edifications concerning the theology and practice of this or that church. A manner of expounding the differences should be noted in particular for its tactfulness and respect for the traditions of churches making this part of the paper a remarkable example of how differences may be discussed and compared ecumenically. Deserving attention is the method of using biblical texts and the reference to the Tradition and liturgical practice of the early Church. It should be noted that the text would have been even more convincing if these references were based on the appropriate patristic assertions. The laconic phrases of the precisely clear exposition reveal the heart of the problems connected with mutual recognition of Baptism, Eucharist and Ministry. One can see the immense work behind every line of the agreed text, the work which took in reflections, research and discussions in the churches which found their expression in the collective wisdom of the members of the Faith and Order Commission.

3. I would like to make a general positive remark and to mention the significance of the distinction made in the Preface between theological convergence and true consensus in faith. This distinction leads to the correct understanding of the unity which is based not on the theological formulations, but on the unity in faith, sacramental life, spiritual experience, witness and service.

"The faith of the church throughout the centuries" rather than a confessional criterion suggested for the evaluation of the document also deserves appreciation. If we understand under this faith the faith of the early undivided Church, it means a very correct methodological step to further improvement of the agreement on Baptism, Eucharist and Ministry.

---

[1] A tendency to reach theological consensus on Baptism, Eucharist and Ministry found a positive evaluation in the report of the Holy Synod Commission on Christian Unity and Interchurch Relations (1977) which was an official response of the Russian Orthodox Church to the Accra document.

4. The Lima document stands out among common ecumenical documents for many reasons. First of all, it touches upon the problems which are the focus of the theological differences and makes an attempt to reach an agreement on the most important questions of faith. The reception of this document by the churches presupposes actions with decisive consequences for their inner life. Secondly, the importance of the document is increased by the fact that it has been unanimously received by a group of theologians who formally represent their churches in the Faith and Order Commission. And thirdly, it was composed and accepted by the representatives of practically all Christian confessions including those which do not belong to the WCC but are nevertheless members of the Faith and Order Commission. In other words, *the BEM document reflects a very high degree of agreement reached on important questions of faith among the widest possible range of ecumenical audiences with official representatives.*

5. All this gives a special authority to the text and calls for thorough attention and respect for it. Yet, in spite of all the importance of the BEM document it is quite clear that it is not a "consensus" on Baptism, Eucharist and Ministry, i.e., it does not reflect full doctrinal agreement. The text is a declaration with an exposition of convergence reached by a group of theologians, but not a declaration of the churches. The agreement does not embrace all problems which exist among the churches on questions of Baptism, Eucharist and Ministry. Implied is an interim provisional character of the Lima statement which serves as a basis for a new theological agreement at a higher level. One may only hope that a new statement would embody responses from the churches to the Lima text and cover all problems which are still not agreed upon. Here I would like to recall a statement from the Preface that consensus is understood as "experience of life and articulation of faith necessary to realize and maintain the Church's visible unity . . . Full consensus can only be proclaimed after the churches reach the point of living and acting together in unity." In light of this statement the Lima document looks like an important link in the chain of the complex process of the churches' consensus on Baptism, Eucharist and Ministry, a process which implies not only theological agreements and verbal overcoming of differences but also an appropriate internal development in the churches which would heal dissensions and bring about genuine consensus.

As to the status of the Lima document, it should be emphasized that regardless of its special authority and significance for the ecumenical movement it has the same status as any other theological agreement reached in the framework of the WCC clearly defined by the principles of the Toronto Declaration and cannot have any other in virtue of the World Council of Churches' nature. In other words, the Lima agreement has no ecclesiological status because neither the Faith and Order Commission nor the WCC can give such a status to it. An ecclesiological status may be given to such documents only by the churches themselves acting together or separately. Obviously, the latter mode of action is already now possible in principle. If this or that church sees an adequate expression of its faith in the Lima document, it can accept it using its innate valid procedure.[2] The ecclesiological status given to the document would have a significance only for this church. As to common reception of the doctrinal documents elaborated on the ecumenical basis by the churches as well as to an ecclesiological status given to them, such an action seems impossible in the WCC framework in principle, since the WCC does not have an ecclesiological reality by virtue of its nature and is just an instrument at the service of the churches striving to achieve unity. And if at one particular historical moment the churches undertake such an action, it would mean that the World Council of Churches ceased to exist and that the Ecumenical Council (Sobor) acts instead.

The lack of the ecclesiological status in no way diminishes the ecumenical significance of the BEM document. This lack only testifies to the reality of the WCC and the Faith and Order Commission.

6. At present the Lima document is being scrutinized and thoroughly analyzed along theological lines by many churches. It is understood that the results of this work would influence the process of its reception. This process has two aspects—external and internal—and it is very important to take both of them into account during theological consideration of the Lima text. When we speak about the internal aspect we mean a critical attitude to our own practice in the light of the provisions of the document which reflect the indubitable truth of the apostolic tradition and the norms of life of the early undivided Church.[3] For many churches this document should become an impetus for the inner theological and liturgical renewal. The external aspect implies the continuation of common efforts undertaken for the solution of the yet unsolved theological problems and for the further growing together in one ecumenical fellowship. Let us consider these problems upon the solution of which the reception of the BEM document depends, as it seems, and which concern both external and internal aspects of the process.

---

[2] This mode of action cannot be used by the local Orthodox Churches, since they compose one Church and have no right to make separate decisions on the doctrinal questions which concern the Orthodox plenitude.

[3] This does not mean a literal repetition of the practice of the early Church, which is impossible in most cases, but a creative use of the norms of life and ministry of the undivided Church under present circumstances.

Baptism

1. This part of the Lima text as well as that of the Accra document is characterized by a greater consent than others. Deserving deep appreciation are an approach to the problem of infant baptism and an openness to an idea of the unity of the three sacraments of initiation: baptism, chrismation and eucharist. Yet, this unity is not reflected in the document as explicitly as would be wished by the Orthodox who, on the one hand, assert a special meaning of each of the three sacraments and, on the other hand, emphasize the necessity of their sequence and perception as total for full initiation. Initiation cannot be considered complete if one of these sacraments is not administered. It is also known that the Orthodox strictly follow the sequence of these sacraments (baptism-chrismation-eucharist) having strong arguments for it which, unfortunately, were not properly reflected in the commentaries. That excludes an opportunity to give a proper evaluation to the Orthodox practice according to which infants are allowed to receive Holy Communion immediately after baptism and chrismation. Actually, it is this practice that most visibly shows the inner unity of the sacraments of initiation. Concerning the western practice of confirmation of children as teenagers and of giving Holy Communion after baptism but before confirmation which pursues the goals of catechizing and provides a personal contact of the initiated persons with their bishop, it is a less visible sign of the unity of the three sacraments. These differences pose serious questions to both sides. How can the Orthodox, while keeping the undoubtedly more correct practice, ensure proper catechization of children and form in them, when they reach the "age of conciousness," a sufficiently responsible attitude to participation in the sacramental life of the Church? And on the other hand, how could the West tie up the fully developed tradition of catechetical instruction with such a practice of initiation which would not shade the inner unity of the three sacraments?

2. The BEM formulations concerning chrismation should be defined more precisely in the future. While declaring that baptism is baptism in water and the Holy Spirit, the document establishes a link between the paschal mystery of death and resurrection and the Pentecostal gift in affirming that "baptism in its full meaning signifies and effects both" (14). Thus an exclusion of a special action through which the gifts of the Holy Spirit are given is allowed. This assertion does not give an answer to the question about the meaning of the passages in the Bible which tell us about the grace of the Holy Spirit descending on the baptized through the laying on of hands on them at the time of the Apostles (Acts 8.15-17) and does not take into account the testimony given by the Tradition of the early Church which had not

been argued until the sixteenth century.

3. Recognizing both the "baptism of infants" and the "baptism of believers," the Lima document rightly emphasizes that they "take place in the Church as the community of faith" and that "the whole congregation reaffirms its faith in God and pledges itself to provide an environment of witness and service" for a baptized person (12). This assertion should be singled out particularly since it contains the truth which could serve as a real basis for mutual recognition of the validity of both forms of baptism and for stopping the practice of rebaptism. But at the same time this assertion contains a challenge for the Orthodox causing them to ponder over the existing practice critically. The same may be said about para. 16 which calls the churches to "guard themselves against the practice of apparently indiscriminate baptism and take more seriously their responsibility for the nurture of the baptized children." Indeed, baptism belongs to the whole Church. It is not a private affair but that of the whole Christian community through which it renews its baptismal vows and takes upon itself responsibility for a baptized person. The importance of baptism was emphasized in the early Church by its celebration at the great feasts—Easter, Pentecost and Epiphany. Such practice corresponds to the very meaning of the sacrament. From the pastoral point of view it would seem very useful to restore this practice at least partly.[4] Thus, for example, the adults could prepare themselves for baptism on special days through receiving the catechetical instruction, as was the case with the early Church. In this connection it would seem quite appropriate to reestablish the institution of catechumens. We have a reminder of it in the Litany of the Catechumens in the Orthodox liturgy and in a special order before baptism. In case of an adult's conversion to the Church it would be more appropriate to perform an order for catechumens and to time baptism to one of the great feasts of the Church. The period of time between the order for catechumens and baptism may be used for the catechetical instruction. In this case it would be only proper to revive the Litany of the Catechumens in those churches which do not use it and thus to express a prayerful care of the congregation for those who prepare themselves for baptism. The very act of baptism performed in the liturgical assembly and combined with the eucharist would not be a private, but a common celebration involving the whole congregation in the renewal of its baptismal vows.

But a priest should keep in mind this communal dimension of the

---

[4] Full restoration of this practice is impossible in many places because of the large number of baptisms, mainly infant baptisms. Some parishes of the Russian Orthodox Church have over ten baptisms a day. On Sundays this number increases considerably.

sacrament even with the existing practice of baptism. His duty is to remind all those present of their own baptism as well as of their responsibility for a baptized person, especially in the case of infant baptism which initiates the catechizing of a new member of the Church.

Eucharist

The Lima document on the Eucharist is a serious step forward in comparison with the Accra document. It is a happy attempt to reach an agreement while leaving behind all differences originated by Scholasticism, Reformation and Counterreformation. It may be asserted that there is the biblical and patristic approach in the paper, though it does not include direct quotations from the holy Fathers.

1. The section "The Eucharist as Anamnesis or Memorial of Christ" should be singled out. While stressing the uniqueness and unrepeatability of the sacrifice of Christ and all that he has accomplished in his incarnation, life, death, resurrection and ascension, the document warns against two delusions: on the one hand, against the thinking that the eucharist can be repeated or prolonged as that sacrifice and those events (8), and on the other hand, against the understanding of anamnesis as a mental recollection or a certain excursus into the past. In the eucharist memorial "Christ himself with all he has accomplished for us . . . is present . . . granting us communion with himself" (6). It is desirable that this important part of the text be more clear and convincing. It should speak explicitly about the action of the Holy Spirit and state clearly that *anamnesis is essentially inseparable from epiklesis.* The Holy Spirit in the eucharist actualizes that which Christ has performed once and forever. The eucharist exists as the sacrament of Christ himself and through it—by the power of the Holy Spirit—members of the Church are really incorporated into Christ and become co-participants in the history of salvation. The eucharist does not *show* this history (as it was and is interpreted by Orthodox upholders of the visual symbolism); it neither continues it, nor reminds of it, but in the sacramental anamnesis we really and truly become the co-participants in the history of salvation. The reality of the sacrament may exist only in the Holy Spirit. Therefore any separation of anamnesis from epiklesis as well as an attempt to bind both exclusively to certain moments of the sacrament (which means to separate them from each other) are inadmissible. The Lima document clearly avoids such separation (14). It would be desirable to have the text composed in such a way as to make this thought well emphasized and the action of the Holy Spirit clearly expounded in the section "Eucharist as Anamnesis . . . "

2. Commentary (8) invites "to review the old controversies about 'sacrifice' in the light of the biblical conception of memorial." The point

is in the concept of "propitiatory sacrifice" used in Catholic theology. This proposal should be welcomed. Yet it is quite important in this connection to analyze thoroughly the use of the term "sacrifice" by the holy Fathers (in *Adversus Haereses* by Saint Irenaios of Lyons, in the appropriate writings of Saint Cyril of Jerusalem, Saint Cyril of Alexandria and by the Fathers of the later period). On the other hand, a question should be posed: whether it is possible, in the light of the same biblical understanding of memorial, to call the eucharist "the sign of his sacrifice" (5), even though "the living and effective sign"? Is this term sufficient for the description of the reality which is revealed in the sacrament, the partaking of which is the central moment in the life of a Christian?

Practically the same may be said about para. 15 in which the bread and wine are called "the sacramental signs of Christ's body and blood." To what extent are such words allowed in the text which solemnly proclaims that "the Church confesses Christ's real, living and active presence in the Eucharist" (13)?[5] Such an unfortunate term as "sign" gives the impression of being a foreign body and its inclusion in the text contradicts both the logic and contents of the document and causes confusion with reason.

3. The Lima document leaves two questions unanswered. The first is mentioned in commentary (13), the second in para. 32. What is meant is the understanding of the reality of Christ's presence in the bread and wine and the practice of reserving the consecrated elements after the sacrament. The manner of speaking about the existing differences should be encouraged. Yet, the very fact of these differences testifies the necessity of further efforts aimed at the elaboration of a fuller theological agreement.

4. The Lima document contains a positive tendency to establish a link between the eucharist and the Church (19), but from the Orthodox point of view it seems necessary to find a more resolute expression of this link. The believers receive baptism in order to become one body (1 Cor 12.13). When the Church celebrates the eucharist it becomes itself, realizing that which it is—the Body of Christ (1 Cor 10.17). *In the eucharist the Church is revealed as the sacramental image of Christ (τρόπος). In this sacramental image his God-man person exists and acts in the history beginning from Pentecost and ending with Parousia.* On the other hand, it may be said that the eucharist creates the Church,

---

[5] The term "real presence" was not known in the patristic tradition. But this is no reason for avoiding its use in a dialogue with the non-Orthodox. Yet, in order to avoid ambiguity it would be helpful in the future to elaborate on a common ecumenical understanding of it or to find an adequate substitute for this term.

since it is in the eucharist that the Holy Spirit makes the Church the Body of Christ. Therefore the eucharist is called the sacrament of the Church. The Church will administer this sacrament until the end of its earthly pilgrimage.

Naturally, the eucharist as the sacrament of the Church implies the participation only of the church members in it. The catechumens were not allowed to stay at the eucharist in the early Church. They left the congregation after the reading of the holy Scriptures and the sermon. The penitents, i.e. those who fell away from the Church through their sins, did not participate in the eucharist either. The eucharist has always been received as a sacrament of communion, as a sacrament of the unity of the Church. On these grounds the Orthodox do not accept the practice of ecumenical intercommunion. There may be only communion in the eucharist, and any intercommunion which implies the participation of persons from outside is excluded by virtue of its nature. That is why the participation in the eucharist is preceded by the confession of faith which testifies to the doctrinal unity of thought of the members of the congregation. There could be no sacrament of the eucharist without unity in faith.

5. Differences in the theological understanding of the eucharist brought about a situation in the past when different churches did not give the same place in their liturgical practice to it: some celebrated it every day, others only on Sundays and on feast days, still others— once a month or even less frequently. The Lima document affirms that it is necessary to celebrate the eucharist ''at least every Sunday'' (31) and encourages every Christian to receive communion frequently. This assertion fully accords with the Orthodox view and poses serious questions the answers to which need a critical evaluation of the existing practice concerning Holy Communion both in the Orthodox and non-Orthodox churches. What is the meaning of the preparation for the Lord's Supper? What place in this preparation is occupied by penitence and asceticism on the necessity of which the Orthodox East has always insisted referring to the warning of Saint Paul (1 Cor 11.27)? And on the other hand, how can we proclaim the central place of the eucharist in the life of the Church restricting ourselves only to the presence at its celebration and partaking of Holy Communion only several times a year? Those who adhere to this practice voluntarily excommunicate themselves from the Church and place themselves outside it, invoking, generally, ''pious'' arguments concerning the necessity of proper preparation. The early Church did not know such a practice of self-excommunication at least until the fourth to fifth centuries. Excommunicated from the eucharist were those who, having committed a sin, did not repent. Originally those were the so-called fallen persons, i.e.

those who could not bear the brunt and trials of persecutions and fell away from the Church.[6] They composed a special group of believers— the penitents. They did not participate in the eucharist while preparing themselves for reconciliation with the community. This reconciliation has been always perceived by the church's conscience as a sacramental act. After receiving forgiveness the penitents came back to the eucharistic community, became its members again and regained the right to participate in the Lord's Supper. The holy sacrament of confession which exists in the Orthodox Church is the sacramental act through which a person who fell away from the eucharistic community through a sin reunites with it. This meaning is revealed in the prayer which is offered during the rite of confession: ". . . reconcile and unite him (her) unto thy holy Church, through Jesus Christ our Lord." Unfortunately, this church community dimension of the confession is supplanted in the consciousness of many Orthodox by a personal dimension. The sacrament is perceived as related exclusively to the person of the penitent and as a spiritual healing given only to him through the remission of sins. But as a sacrament of the reunion with the Church confession *heals the divisions in the community,* constantly recreating unity around the Lord's Table. In the modern practice of confession the Orthodox have two, rather widespread extremes. One consists in very rare administering of this sacrament. Mentioned here in the first place should be the ministers many of whom make their confession just one or two times a year. The other extremity finds its expression in the firmly rooted connection between confession and every participation in the eucharist. In the case of regular and frequent communion it leads to formalism, to the practice of receiving an absolution prayer. Thus confession becomes a kind of pass for those wishing to come to the holy chalice. Neither of these extremes facilitates eucharistic piety, i.e. the regular participation in the eucharist with the proper spiritual preparation. The Orthodox Churches face a great and difficult task: how, while encouraging the practice of frequent communion, to provide conditions for our contemporaries necessary for spiritual and moral preparation for the eucharist. It seems quite probable that this problem may be solved if the meaning and sense of the confession for the spiritual life of a believer and the whole community are restored in accordance with the norms of the early Church and if pastors adapt the unbroken principles of Christian asceticism to the conditions of the present times. In this field the Orthodox may render an invaluable service to other churches, thus promoting the correct implementation of the

---

[6] Hermas in his "Shepherd" speaks about other transgressions which were strictly condemned in the early Christian communities.

recommendations of the Lima document concerning frequent communion.

It should be added to the above-said that the theme of confession must find its worthy place in the ecumenical agreement on the Eucharist.

Ministry

This part of the Lima document is the largest in comparison with the other two. It considers the questions of ecclesiology, church order and practice which lie at the heart of the existing confessional differences. In spite of a remarkable progress in this field since the Accra meeting this part of the document is less agreed upon. Without going into positive aspects of the statement on Ministry we shall touch upon only major controversial problems the solution of which would determine perspectives of the process of reception.

1. The Lima document does not make a sufficiently clear distinction between the ministry of the people of God and the ordained ministry. Correctly affirming the roots of both in the unique priesthood of Christ (17), the text speaks very loosely about the nature of the difference between them.

2. It should also be noted that BEM does not sufficiently bring out the link of succession between the ministry of the Apostles and that of ordained ministers. An assertion that the ministry of ordained ministers is founded on the ministry of the Apostles (10) is general in character and does not explain the nature of the dependence of the former upon the latter. The elucidation of the meaning of this link seems principally important for the understanding of the nature of the ordained ministry. The document quite correctly affirms the uniqueness and unrepeatability of the ministry of the Apostles and the ordained ministers (10). Yet, while emphasizing the difference, it does not say anything about that which is common for both ministries. But this commonness exists and is conditioned by the very mission of the Apostles: they are witnesses of the resurrection (Lk 24.28) who received special power from the Holy Spirit and are called to bear their witness even "to the end of the earth" (Acts 1.8). The ministry of the witness could hardly be restricted to one generation of the eyewitnesses of the Resurrected. It was received by those to whom these eyewitnesses transmitted the right given to them by the Lord to be witnesses. These people may be called, according to Saint Paul, "apostles from men" (Gal 1.1), the apostles who became such through the mediation of the real witnesses of the Risen One. They could not convey the unrepeatable character of the witness of the eyewitnesses to their successors, but they committed their ministry to them, which is to preserve in the Church the very truth of the witness. Saint Paul shares his apostleship with Silvanus,

Timothy and Titus since they are also apostles, though "from men."[7]
They differ from Saint Paul not in the scope of their ministry but in
the extent of their personal authority. The Pastoral Epistles imply a
practical identity of the apostolic activities of Paul and Timothy. Both
perform two important ministries which compose the contents of the
apostleship: mission and management of the organized communities.

Whatever the interpretation of the term "apostle" in the second
century by the theologians, [8] the very fact of the existence of this term
testifies that the early Church saw a successive link between the ministry
of the eyewitnesses of the Resurrected and the ministry in the Christian communities in the post-apostolic time.

To reflect this succession in the ecumenical statement on Ministry
would mean to make a real major advance to the genuine agreement.

From here we should proceed to the very important question of the
apostolic succession. The Lima document differentiates the apostolic
Tradition of the Church from the succession of the apostolic ministry.
This distinction is fair, because the apostolic Tradition means continuity in the permanent characteristics of the Church of the Apostles, including the ministry (commentary 34). Speaking about the realization
of this continuity the Lima document affirms: "Within the Church the
ordained ministry has a particular task of preserving and actualizing
the apostolic faith" (35). Hence the conclusion: "The orderly transmission of the ordained ministry is therefore a powerful expression of the
continuity of the Church throughout history' (35). Therefore "the
succession of bishops became one of the ways . . . in which the apostolic Tradition of the Church was expressed (36). All these formulations should be welcomed, since they mark a major advance in the

---

[7] Thus, in the Epistle to the Thessalonians, Saint Paul wrote that they might claim a
certain authority and power as apostles of Christ (1 Th 2.6). "They" include not only
Paul, but Silvanos and Timothy (1 Th 1.1; 2 Th 1.1). The name of Timothy is met together
with an authoritative signature of Paul in the Epistle to the Philippians (Phil 1.1). The
ministry itself rather than the appellation speaks of the apostleship of Saint Paul's companions. They were the preachers of Jesus Christ, the Son of God (2 Cor 1.19), and
had received this ability from the Lord. God animates them with the Spirit (2 Cor 3.3).
They were "ambassadors for Christ, God making his appeal" through them (2 Cor 5.20)
because they worked together with him (2 Cor 6.1) and were entrusted with the Gospel
(1 Th 2.4). Paul sends his co-workers who share in his apostleship to different communities
in order that they should replace him there and encourage steadfastness in the believers.
It is obvious from the Pastoral Epistles that the closer the time of Paul's departure
(2 Tim 4.6), the more important the ministry of his companions becomes and the more
vividly it is narrated. The Pastoral Epistles tell us about the extensive activities of Paul's
co-workers.

[8] As, for instance, in "The Didache." One of the controversial attempts to explain
the term "apostle" as used in the second century was undertaken by A. Harnack. See
A. Harnack, *Prolegomena, Texte und Untersuchungen,* Bd 2, Heft 1-2, Leipzig, 1884,
s. 112.

agreement on the apostolic succession. Yet, according to the Lima document itself, "Among the issues that need to be worked on . . . that of the apostolic succession is of particular importance" (52). Indeed, the above-mentioned formulations do not solve the problem of the apostolic succession. Moreover, there is an impression that this problem cannot be solved on the level of the Lima document, since it is presented here along the pragmatical lines: the document emphasizes the *activities* of the ministers and speaks about the *task* of a minister "of preserving and actualizing the apostolic faith" (35). It becomes clear in this context why the Lima text avoids speaking of the episcopal succession as one of the guarantees of the continuity of the apostolic Tradition. Indeed, this guarantee can be given neither by the activities of the bishops, nor by their personal qualities, nor by their solution of "the task of preserving and actualizing" the faith. (There were heretics and people unworthy of their ministry among bishops.) The guarantee lies in the apostolic ministry itself, in its charisma. Therefore the problem of the apostolic succession should not be considered on the pragmatic and even less on the anthropological level, but on the ontological one. Apostolic succession is the truth in all its fullness and wholeness. The Church is the custodian of this Truth, the pillar and bulwark of it (1 Tim 3.15). The Truth cannot be either half- or semi-truth. The apostolic Tradition can only be integral. The ministry of the apostles is an ontological part of the Tradition. There is no whole without this part; there is no apostolic Tradition without the apostolic ministry. It would certainly be a mistake to affirm that only the sucession of the apostolic ministry guarantees the wholeness and continuity of the Tradition and ensures the apostolic succession in the Church. It is ensured by the transmission of the apostolic faith and the distinctive characteristics of the apostolic Church, including Baptism, Eucharist and the apostolic Ministry. Distortion of the apostolic faith or loss of any of these characteristics (and not only these) severs the continuity and wholeness of the apostolic Tradition, in other words— disrupts the apostolic succession. As to the preserving of the continuity of the apostolic ministry, it is achieved by the continuity of ordinations performed by those who carry out this ministry, i.e. bishops. Episcopal succession is something more than a mere "sign" of the continuity of the apostolic Tradition (53); similarly the ordination performed by a bishop is not only a tribute to "the old Tradition which should be recognized and respected" (comm. 39).

This is the most important element of the apostolic Tradition conditioned by the very nature of the apostolic ministry: only those can be successors of the apostles who received the right to continue their ministry from the apostles—the eyewitnesses of the Resurrected. The ordination performed by a bishop who stands in the consecutive line of the apostles' successors ensures the link between the ordained and the apostles, i.e. guarantees the receiving of the apostolic ministry. The ordaining bishop is, so to say, a mediator between the apostles—witnesses to the resurrection and the ordained person who receives the charisma of the apostolic ministry. The successive laying on of hands by bishops should not be understood as a mechanical transmission of the charisma. The Lima document correctly asserts that "it is the Risen Lord who is the true ordainer and bestows the gift" (39). Ordination is also the "invocation of the Holy Spirit—epiklesis" (41), implying "the absolute dependence on God for the outcome of the Church's prayer" (42).

The manner in which the Lima document raises the question of the apostolic succession deserves high appreciation. It is necessary to give this important theme a worthy place in the ecumenical discussion in the immediate furture and especially in the context of the search for "The Common Expression of the Apostolic Faith Today."[9]

3. While recognizing special gifts of the Holy Spirit in the ordained minister (41, 42, 44)[10] the Lima document at the same time avoids mentioning the sacramental character of this ministry. It is probably so because the BEM document does not consider the problem of sacraments at all. Speaking about Baptism, Eucharist and Ministry the document says nothing about the sacrament of the Church. This is the main omission, perhaps the weakest point in the whole document. This weakness becomes more tangible in the section "The Church and the Ordained Ministry" which totally lacks the sacramental-ecclesiological dimension. Without understanding the sacramental nature of the Church it is impossible to understand the sacramental character of the ordained ministry either, as witnessed by the Tradition of the early un-divided Church. The same weakness may explain why the connection between Eucharist and Ministry is brought out so insufficiently. A very brief para. 14 and commentary on it say practically nothing about the nature of this connection. It seems absolutely necessary to give a thorough study to the theme of sacraments, because without an ecumenical agreement in this field the significance of the BEM

---

[9] The question of "The Common Expression of the Apostolic Faith Today" is in essence a question of the wholeness, nondistortion and continuity of the apostolic Tradition in the life of the churches at present, i.e. a question of the apostolic succession. Dependent on the solution of this question is the mutual recognition of churches as true churches and the establishment of full communion between them which includes the recognition of ministries.

[10] It would be appropriate here to use the expression "charism of an ordained minister" in accordance with the explanations given in para 7.

document is lessened.

4. The Lima document suggests that the churches should undertake concrete steps for the sake of mutual recognition of ministries. Thus, churches without the episcopal succession are actually called on to recover it (53b). Churches which have preserved the episcopal succession are invited to recognize "both the apostolic content of the ordained ministry which exists in churches which have not maintained such succession and also the existence in these churches of a ministry of episkope in various forms" (53a). And here a question arises: how may such recognition be attained? The hierarchical structure of churches which did not preserve the episcopal succession after the sixteenth century has undergone certain changes which were often introduced with a view to adjust to new conditions and were explained by the testimonies from the New Testament understood in this or that way (cf. 19). But these changes were not realized in line with the apostolic Tradition of the Church, and this is the root of the problem. Such notions as "the apostolic content of the ordained ministry" and "episkope" are those from the apostolic Tradition. Out of the Tradition they lose their true meaning and significance and so they may have any meaning and any significance. There is no guarantee that the meaning and significance will not be changed on account of time, conditions of life and sometimes of theological opinions and tendencies. Even if mutual recognition of the ordained ministries were achieved today, it would be a fiction without a common faithfulness to the apostolic tradition, since already tomorrow it might be cancelled by a new understanding of the ministries or by a radically new practice. Are we not witnessing at present such a new understanding and such a radically new practice in the form of women's priesthood?[11] This invocation gives a convincing example of what could happen if a renewal of the church's life takes place outside the apostolic Tradition: it could lead to new divisions and nullify all efforts aimed at the restoration of unity. The same happened in the past and is happening in the present: ideals of renewal are opposed to the unity of the Church and the choice is made of the former. We see today how the aspirations of millions of Christians for unity and the substantial theological achievements in this field (as, for instance, the BEM document) are disrupted by the introduction of women's

---

[11]The question of women's priesthood, i.e. of giving women a right to celebrate the eucharist should be separated from the problem of women's ministry in the church. The Orthodox should participate most actively in the solving of this problem. It seems important in this context to make a fresh study of the experience of the early Church which gave wide opportunities to women for participation in the life, ministry and witness of a Christian community, and to make a critical evaluation of the church's practice in the light of this experience.

priesthood.[12] And what comes next? What is the sense of agreements if in the future they could be reappraised and reinterpreted separately with ensueing radical practical steps which might break the church's unity? We should strive for doctrinal agreements and aspire for mutual recognition only when the churches agree to use one, common criterion of evaluating the church's life and the efforts undertaken for the sake of unity. The Tradition of the early undivided Church of the times of the Seven Ecumenical Synods may be the only criterion,[13] because this Tradition witnesses to the experience of unity and the struggle for unity for which we are striving. An agreement on the unbroken normative significance of the Tradition of the Seven Ecumenical Synods would become a sure instrument for the achievement of unity and its preservation in the future. Common recognition by the churches of the principles and norms of this Tradition will make any doctrinal agreement real and sustainable—mutual recognition of the ordained ministry included. Moreover, this recognition would guard such agreements against their arbitrary interpretation and against any practical actions which may undermine their meaning for the unity of the Church. Concerning a proposal from para. 53a (to recognize the apostolic ministry and episkope in the churches which have not maintained the episcopal succession) it would be possible to accept it only on condition that the norms of the Tradition of the undivided Church be used. Using these norms, it would be possible to decide to what extent these churches have preserved the apostolic ministry and episkope and which further steps are necessary for the mutual recognition of the ordained ministry.[14]

5. The Lima document poses a question to the Orthodox which may be fomulated as follows: to what extent does the modern practice of the ministry of bishops, presbyters and deacons allow the realization of their potential for the most effective witness of the Church in this world (25)? Indeed, how can the Orthodox who maintain the principles of conciliarity (sobornost) realize them today with greater effectiveness, showing in practice the unity of the episcopate, clergy and all believers

---

[12]Suffice it to mention the repeated appeals of the upholders of women's priesthood to introduce it in spite of all ecumenical arguments in order to realize the danger of this innovation for the search of Christian unity.

[13]A reference to the Oriental Orthodox Churches (pre-Chalcedonian) usually made by the non-Orthodox opponents to the normative character of the time of the seven Ecumenical Synods is erroneous in essence. The Oriental Orthodox Churches, while not recognizing all these synods formally, practically share common Tradition with the Eastern Orthodox Churches. This was stated clearly at the Joint Consultation in Geneva in 1970.

[14]The same should be said about the acceptance of the episcopal succession by the churches which do not have it. This acceptance would have a decisive meaning for the unity of the Church if it is realized in accordance with the apostolic tradition and the norms of life of the undivided Church.

in the solution of problems facing the Church? How may these principles be effectively developed on the Pan-Orthodox level and facilitate
the overcoming of difficulties and misunderstandings which appeared
as a result of the historical development of Orthodoxy? Finally, how
far does the present content of these ministries with all their functions
correspond to our knowledge about them derive from the history of
the Church?[15] Obviously, this list does not exhaust the questions which
face the Orthodox in connection with the Lima statement on Ministry.

* * * * *

A person who is familiar with the BEM document does not have
any doubts about its particular significance both for the ecumenical
movement as a whole and for the churches which participate in it, including the Orthodox Churches. Despite controversial and unagreed
parts, the Lima text is the most successful compared with previous attempts to reach an ecumenical agreement on the important doctrinal
questions. Differences stated in the document show the reality of the
divisions among churches rather than the weakness of the text. But the
BEM document suggests methodology, terminolgy and formulations
which provide an opportunity for the continuation of a constructive
theological dialogue. In other words, the Lima document gives a good
basis for further theological work within the churches and among them,
including bilateral and multilateral conversations in the framework of
the ecumenical movement.

The true meaning of the BEM document will be shown by life itself.
If this document is able to bring about real changes in the theology
and practice of the churches with the aim of reviving the norms of life
of the early undivided Church and if, as a result of this revival, the
churches come to a true consensus on Baptism, Eucharist and Ministry,
then its historical mission will be fulfilled. But the real development
does not depend on the Lima document or any other ecumenical document. It depends on the churches and their desire and abilty to structure their life and to fulfill their ministry in such a way as to imple-
ment creatively the principles of life and minsitry of the early undivided
Church in conditions of the present time. The Orthodox have a lot to
say in this regard, for, according to an outstanding Russian theologian,
"the creative revival of the Orthodox world is a necessary condition
for the solution of the 'ecumenical problem.' "[16]

---

[15]Thus, for instance, the functions of deacons which at one time included administrative and charitable duties are reduced to assistance to a bishop or priest during
divine services.

[16]Archpriest G. Florovsky, *Ways of Russian Theology,* Paris, 1937, p. 516.

The BEM Document in Romanian Orthodox Theology: The Present Stage of Discussions

METROPOLITAN ANTONIE PLĂMĂDEALĂ

THE BEM DOCUMENT (Baptism, Eucharist and Ministry: Convergence in the Faith) presented at Lima in 1982, has been received with much interest by theologians in Romania, even with a certain degree of enthusiasm and with optimistic expectations. It was examined at three *interconfessional conferences* (at Sibiu on May 18, 1978—the Accra version of 1974, and on May 17, 1984 and November 27, 1984—the Lima text) and by several though not many theologians who wrote about it.

The theme has somehow taken many by surprise and the feeling of surprise still persists. One would say: *It is too nice to be true!* and on the other hand: *It is too daring to get used to it at once!* After so many centuries of separation, suddenly before us stands a surprising, almost unbelievable formula of unity, particularly so as it comes from the Protestants. These were responses given at the first reading of the text. After a second reading, our theologians have compared their Orthodox faith with the the proposals put forward by the document and after examining them have discovered the differences which still persist. Nobody could agree with what the document *changes, innovates* and *interprets* in ways different from one's own traditional interpretation. Nevertheless, all have seen an invitation to reflection coming out of the formulas of the document and have expressed their hope that these formulas will be deepened both in the light of their common theological tradition—the one prior to the separation—and in the light of possible reinterpretations of the post-separation traditions of the confessions engaged in dialogue.

In what follows we shall attempt to make an assessment of the present stage of discussions on the BEM document in Romanian theology.

In fact, the first thing which gave rise to difficulties was the term *convergence* in the title of the document. What does *convergence* in matters of faith and doctrine mean? How far can convergence which is not identity go? What does convergence imply? Does it imply a common faith expressed in different formulas? Or on the contrary: a common formula for an article of faith but having different contents? These seem to be of both kinds. Since there are many ambiguities in the language of the document, the suggested convergences must be studied one by one, clarified, and then put forward for agreement. No step further can be taken before a clarification of and agreement on the language.

Theologians in Romania have not yet studied all the problems which raise such difficulties. One that has been debated refers to the term *Ministry* in the title of the document. What does it mean for the Orthodox and what does it mean for the Protestants? Does it mean the same thing? Does it have the same content? At a superficial and very general look the answer would be: yes. But when one proceeds to define concretely its content, he finds that the Orthodox give it one meaning, while the Protestants another. The translator of the document into Romanian was, naturally, confronted with this difficulty. After consultation with other theologians and even with several hierarchs, it was decided to translate *Ministry* (or *Ministere* in the French version) with *Slujire* (Service). The reason given for the selection of that term was that in a Protestant understanding and in the meaning given it by the authors of the document, *Ministry* is not limited to a sacerdotal priesthood, one based on ordination and apostolic succession, but it is more encompassing, containing also the priesthood of the believers and the social diakonia. This is exactly what *Ministry* means: ministerium, service. The Romanian translator wanted to give a faithful rendering of the word as it is currently understood by Protestants. It remains to be seen whether or not he made the right choice. But it is not the meaning of *Ministry* as service which interests us. We think that we have dialogued and must continue to dialogue in the document about *the sacrament of priesthood* and not about service in general. The Protestants may believe that we approve of their "priesthood" as Orthodox priesthood, when we actually approve only of their service in general in the form of preaching, missionary action and charitable institutions, etc. Our theologians have stated that on service in general we can easily agree. Things change when we come to the aspect of Ministry as priesthood. Convergence on this aspect must be defined as such and beyond any ambiguity.

Priesthood is not only diminished by the term *Ministry,* but also totally counterfeited. It is something else. Something that stems from the general mandate of all Christians, or from the mandate of a community and not from a sacramental institution. In that case, as has been noted by some theologians, *Baptism* and *Eucharist* would also be greatly shadowed since they would be performed by a non-sacramental priesthood.

In general, sacramental priesthood is not sufficiently dealt with in the document. Discussion on that issue took up a good part of the inter-confessional conference held in Bucharest on November 27, 1984. If we acknowledge *Ministry* to be equal with *Slujire* (Service) we can agree with the text and can easily achieve convergence with the Protestants, but then we would not speak about *the sacrament of priesthood* but about something totally different. Such convergences would be false convergences. It has therefore been required to first clarify the terms that are being used in the document. If we stick to *Ministry,* a term with such a wide range of connotations in the languages of the West and with a certain degree of ambiguity even in those languages, the term would have to be very clearly defined *even for Westerners,* so that they may know about what they are actually talking, and avoid furthering false convergences. The term *Ministry,* for example, could also encompass, in its broader meaning, the so-called ministry of women, on which a convergence could finally be reached, but if we speak about priesthood as sacrament, the service of women is no longer part of the term.

A clarification of terms is also a question of honesty. False impressions should be avoided. Convergence, when it is achieved, must be a real convergence. Otherwise, it would not reach farther than a conference room. It would not be received since the people of God would not receive ambiguous formulas.

One of the interconfessional conferences in Romania dealt also with the problem of *reception.* As it stands now, as a text on which convergence is to be reached—since it is not yet a text of convergence—the BEM document cannot be forwarded for reception by the churches in the sense in which the items of faith have been received in history. There is an impropriety about the term *reception* as it is being used in BEM. The document is subject to *discussion,* not to reception. We can talk about its authentic reception *only* after it has been given a definitive form and it has been accepted at a pan-Orthodox level, if we would reach that stage, and if our Protestant and Roman Catholic partners would also subscribe to the same text.

A request for its reception *now* would mean to anticipate *yes* and *no* responses as in a referendum. But this cannot be asked even from a conference or a symposium. The document is being discussed now in view not of its reception but of its improvement, and in order to methodically achieve a step by step, chapter by chapter convergence.

Reception will follow in the end and will be achieved through well-known and historically validated means, so that any discussion of it now would be premature.

I have mentioned these things here since they took up a good part of the discussions on BEM in the interconfessional conferences in Romania.

The Romanian Orthodox theologians have also proceeded to do an analysis of the document itself.

1. With respect to Baptism they have discovered many points of convergence but have nevertheless also noticed a few ambiguous sentences, which, if worked out, would gain greater clarity. Not all of the latter pertain to fundamental doctrinal issues. Several theologians have come up with more serious objections. They regard the term *sign* used in relation to baptism as not being a good choice. There are *signs* also in the Orthodox Church's baptism. The water, oil, the ritual gestures can be *signs, symbols,* but baptism is not just a symbol. It is also a sacrament, an incorporation into Christ, therefore something greater and of a different nature. BEM also speaks of an "incorporation" into the Body of Christ, but it does not properly connect *sign* with *incorporation.*

Our theologians have also found a certain openness towards the sacrament of chrismation, or confirmation, one that is greater than that existing in the Accra version (1974). Nevertheless, as it is being presented in the current text, the sacrament of chrismation is absorbed by the sacrament of baptism, which fact represents a divergence from the Orthodox doctrine.

In relation to Baptism, the document speaks about "the ministry of Jesus of Nazareth." Some Romanian theologians regard the use of this expression here as being inadequate, since it suggests a Bultmannian discontinuity between "Jesus of Nazareth" and "Christ the Lord."

2. With respect to Eucharist, appreciation has been expressed for the general importance given to the sacrament, as a sacrament, and for the recognition of its place in the center of Christian life and for salvation. Criticism has been voiced about the great emphasis on *justification* which is *external* and *forensic* as an act of *satisfaction* brought to the Father. The exclusive *memorial* character of the Eucharist has also been disapproved of since the emphasis is actually on *anamnesis.* Others have spoken critically about the fact that there is here an understanding of the sinner as becoming through the Eucharist a *justified sinner,* and therefore not completely restored, not being the subject of an ontological transformation which makes him not a *justified sinner* but a new, a renewed creature. Criticism was also expressed about the fact that although the document speaks of a real presence of Christ in the eucharistic elements, the theory of impanation (*in pane, cum*

pane, sub pane) still persists. The bread and wine remain sacramental signs of the Body and Blood of Christ.

Objections have also been raised with respect to a lack of relation between eucharist and confession which if present here could lead to consensus on the sacrament of penance.

Roman Orthodox theologians believe that is possible to overcome these shortcomings through greater clarity and through a balancing of the document with the help of correct Orthodox statements which are abundantly present in the text. This is possible since the document does not omit the Orthodox affirmation of faith, but in order to also satisfy the Protestants, it attempts to make adjustments commensurate with certain Protestant theories. Even though it cannot remain in its present form, this document represents a praiseworthy ecumenical effort.

As in the case of Baptism, the use of the term *sign* in the text of BEM in relation to Eucharist is regarded as being ambiguous. More appropriate would be terms such as *element, matter, gesture.* These terms cannot be misinterpreted from a dogmatic point of view. As a matter of fact, the term *sign* is too frequently used throughout the document.

The statement according to which in the eucharist one receives "the assurance of the forgiveness of sins" is believed to be evasive. Why is it not stated more simply and in the words of the Scripture: "for the forgiveness of sins." The same theologians, however, note with satisfaction the unambiguous affirmation of the real presence of Christ in the eucharist. In this light, the addition of its meaning as *memorial* can be accepted. Any ambiguity about this term is removed by its translation into Romanian as *pomenire.*

According to some Romanian theologians, the role and action of the Holy Spirit has been insufficiently shown in BEM with respect to all the three sacraments. For example, they find BEM to follow the western tradition when affirming that the transformation of the gifts in the eucharist takes place when the words of institution are being uttered and not as is the case with us, through the invocation of the Holy Spirit. The Lord's suffering, sacrifice, death and resurrection occurred *after* the institution of the eucharist at the Last Supper and therefore not when the words of institution were spoken. The eucharist is the presence of Christ who suffers, is sacrificed, dies and rises from the dead. *The Last Supper* and the above events were not concomitant. These problems are not elucidated in the fourteenth chapter of the Eucharist section of BEM on *the Eucharist as invocation of the Spirit.* The final part of the section on Eucharist has also been objected to by Romanian theologians since it ushers in "the obsolete formula of intercommunion" prior to the achievement of unity in the faith.

3. The chapter on Ministry also contains theses which are not accepted by Romanian theologians. They do not agree with the fact that at the ordination of a priest, room is also left for the instituting (ordaining) role of the community, even though the ordination performed by the bishop is acknowledged in the document.

The community is also present in the Orthodox ritual having to answer when the bishop asks if the candidate "is worthy," but it is not the community that performs the ordination. Some theologians believe that if at the ordination the essential role of the bishop is acknowledged and maintained, the BEM text may be regarded as convergent in this respect.

Still others see in the text, which states that *the Church institutes* the priesthood, a new and veiled form of *the mandate of the community* for which reason they suggest that any ambiguity should be avoided.

Objections have also been raised about those passages in BEM which affirm that the churches that possess apostolic succession recognize continuity in apostolic faith, worship and missionary action to the churches that have not maintained an episcopate of apostolic succession. This would represent a lessening of the importance of apostolic succession. A reconciliation with us has been considered unacceptable in such conditions of ambiguity. "Continuity in apostolic faith" is different from "apostolic succession." Otherwise it should be explicitly stated that they are one and the same thing. The general priesthood of the believers (1 Pet 2.5-9), as is known, is not rejected by the Orthodox, but when it comes to the realization of Christ in the sacrament, that is being done through the sacrament of priesthood. This also gives meaning to the "priesthood" of the believers.

It has therefore been concluded that the BEM document is still hesitant with respect to the priesthood, to "the ordained ministry" in contrast to that which is called "general." For example, the document attempts to derive the ordained ministry, the sacramental priesthood, from the general priesthood of the believers. It says that the churches should take as starting point "the calling of the whole people of God." But we rather start from Jn 15.16: "You did not choose me; I chose you." That is why a theologian has written: "There is no question of a *priesthood* in BEM. Its sacramental aspect is undecipherable and the predominantly descriptive character of the text with its numerous consolidations of Protestant positions shows that a forthcoming common formulation of the theme is not in sight."

Our theologians have objected to the opinion of the BEM document on the threefold form of the priesthood of which it says that it has not always been present in the Church, but has been the outcome of an evolution, and the Church has the ability to restructure it. We know that it was already present in the New Testament and in the writings of the apostolic Fathers. The question of restructuring it could regard only the Protestants.

Objections have also been stated about the opinions on the ordination of women, which opinions are too vague and leave the impression that the Orthodox have introduced an innovation by leaving it aside in the course of history.

On the other hand, Romanian theologians have expressed satisfaction with the great progress achieved through the Lima text.

Evidently, as Professor Nikos Nissiotis warned, no one should try to find in BEM one's own confessional faith (Geneva, July 1982). But during the time in which we still discuss, all of us must judge from the standpoint of our own confession. Even afterwards the document would have to correspond to our own confession and we would expect of it *the miracle* of corresponding also to the conscience of our partners in dialogue as they themselves would expect of us the same miracle. That is why the document must be made to be *everybody's,* no matter how difficult that may be. It would have to be everybody's or nobody's. There is no other alternative. Only as such it would not give rise to any triumphalism.

As has been noticed, in this presentation I brought up only a few points of convergence and consensus noted by Romanian theologians. There are, however, many more. It would have been interesting to deal with them also, but I thought it more useful to present the objections. Convergences will stand out by themselves. Divergences must be pointed out in order to solve them together with our partners of other confessions. They themselves will undoubtedly communicate to us their own divergences. Those we will have to examine again and only then make good use of our convergences and defend them.

Generally speaking, the Romanian Orthodox theologians consider the BEM document to be a major step forward and a courageous expression of the desire and hope for unity of all Christians. (The present assessment has taken into consideration views on BEM expressed by: His Eminence Metropolitan Nicolae Corneanu, Professors D. Stăniloae, I. Ică, I. Bria, D. Popescu, D. Radu, I. Fleca, Assistant Professor I. Sauca, Anca Manolache, and this speaker.)

For the answer to be sent to the World Council of Churches, the Romanian Patriarchate has set up a Commission made up of Metropolitan Antonie Plămădeală of Transylvania, Metropolitan Nicolae Corneanu of the Banat, and the following professors: Dumitru Stăniloae, Dumitru Radu, Constantin Galeriu and Stefan Alexe of Bucharest, Ioan Ică and Ioan Fleca of Sibiu. The Commission will present its observations to the fall 1985 session of the Holy Synod of the Romanian Orthodox Church. The conclusions of this conference will also be available and they will certainly be useful to us.

The Question of the Reception of BEM in the Orthodox Church in the Light of its Ecumenical Commitment

THEODORE STYLIANOPOULOS

A FEW INTRODUCTORY COMMENTS on points raised by the title of this paper are necessary. First, I took the liberty of changing my own original title by using the singular "Orthodox Church" rather than the plural "Orthodox Churches," in order to underscore the unity of the Orthodox Church. While the plural certainly carries its own legitimacy, ecumenical discourse today seems increasingly to favor the plural, expressing an ecclesiological ambiguity which needs to be clarified. I discuss this matter in the last section of this paper.

Secondly, by reception I do not signify that ecclesial process through which the Orthodox Church has received the authoritative decrees of Ecumenical Synods or continues to receive today the decisions of the canonical synods of Orthodox bishops. Although this process itself is in some ways instructive to the question at hand, clearly BEM neither presupposes nor claims that kind of ecclesial authority. By reception I mean rather the general process of any tradition engaging, either from within or from without, new ideas, acts or practices, which are consciously or unconsciously assessed, and then in various ways accepted or rejected by the living tradition of a people. The most authentic kind of reception involves an active response, a critical reaction to something on the basis of a given tradition's own values. From the beginning of the history of salvation the people of God have inevitably been involved in such a broad, dynamic process regarding laws, customs, forms of worship, teaching, institutions and even the biblical canons—all of which have been subject to variety, revision and evaluation according to the mind of the people of God guided by the Holy Spirit. Critical

105

reception is decisive to authentic renewal: it is the power of a tradition to maintain itself as a living tradition and thereby to be able effectively to witness to its own deepest insights and truths.

And thirdly, one might ask in what way(s) the reception of BEM is a question. The Vancouver Assembly (1983) stated that the Lima text "is at one and the same time a challenge and an opportunity for the churches."[1] Many theologians as well have already written about the new ecumenical moment reached through the publication of BEM by virtue of half a century of patient labor within the Faith and Order Commission of the World Council of Churches. The bold hope of the Faith and Order Commission, according to J. M. R. Tillard, is "to make possible a new and universal Reformation embracing all the Christian traditions—Orthodox, Roman Catholic, as well as Protestant."[2] BEM is indeed a profound question to the divided churches, both stimulating and perplexing, a question which in future years will probe the depth of their ecumenical commitment at the heart of which is the willingness to walk together on the difficult road to unity.

However, in another way the churches have the right to question the question as a normal part of the reception process. That the BEM document has raised the issue of continuing membership in the World Council for some churches is not surprising. During the long process of reception, unless the goal of unity is set aside as unreachable, BEM will ultimately raise the same issue for all the member churches. The reception of BEM in the Orthodox Churches, although having raised no concerns about continuing membership, is nevertheless a matter of question for many complex reasons. One reason is the preliminary confusion over the meaning of reception. Other reasons have to do with the spiritual readiness, the theological vision, and the canonical ecclesiology of the Orthodox Churches.

As a major ecumenical document BEM does obviously not exist in a vacuum but bears the hopes and ambiguities of the whole ecumenical movement. Its reception in the Orthodox Church is intimately related to the ongoing problematic nature of the Orthodox membership in the World Council—with or without BEM—and specifically its own self-understanding of being the one, holy, catholic and apostolic Church, its place in the World Council, and its joys and frustrations arising from ecumenical engagement. As an ecumenical event BEM raises anew the issue of the relationship of the Orthodox Church to the World

---

[1] David Gill, ed., *Gathered for Life: Official Report of the Fourth Assembly of the World Council of Churches* (Geneva-Grand Rapids, 1983), p. 45.

[2] J. M. R. Tillard, "BEM: The Call for a Judgment upon the Churches and the Ecumenical Movement," *Mid-Stream* 23, no. 3 (1984) 237.

Council. My purpose in this paper is to examine some of the most important of the above reasons bearing on the reception of BEM in the Orthodox Churches in three closely related perspectives—spiritual, theological, and ecclesiological. I do so with the prayerful hope that the two-way questions of the reception process of BEM will cause the Orthodox Church both to renew and to deepen its ecumenical commitment in a hopeful and realistic way.

The Spiritual Challenge

The spiritual challenge raised by BEM has several dimensions such as the contents of BEM which have to do with Christian life and not merely with abstract theology, the implications of BEM for the mutual relations between the churches, and the spiritual readiness of any church seriously determining that church's quality of response to BEM. All these dimensions find their focus in the ecumenical reality which we have called a "fellowship of churches." What is the nature and depth of this fellowship? Has this fellowship matured to a point in which it is able to deal positively with BEM that the fellowship might grow deeper and stronger? Some broader remarks about this fellowship might be helpful.

The 1920 Patriarchal Encyclical, the spiritual breath of the ecumenical movement, challenged all the churches, despite their doctrinal differences, to join in a fellowship (*koinonia*)[3] of churches which, on the one hand, would renounce all distrust, bitterness, polemics and proselytism, and, on the other hand, would allow themselves to be rekindled by Christ's love so that the divided churches "should no more consider one another as strangers and foreigners, but as relatives, and as being a part of the household of Christ"[4] (cf. Eph 2.19). Thanks be to God that, beyond anyone's expectation, the hope of the Patriarchal Encyclical, and others as well, have been fulfilled in just over fifty years of ecumenical labor through the one ecumenical movement chiefly represented by the World Council of Churches. The dream of faith is now a reality: "a fellowship of churches which confess the Lord Jesus Christ as God and Savior according the Scriptures and therefore seek to fulfill together their common calling to the glory of the one God, Father, Son and Holy Spirit." This basis of the World Council is not only a constitutional declaration but also a spiritual affirmation. Membership in the World Council is not merely an act of ecclesiastical formality but above all a spiritual act—an act of ecclesial conscience informed by the Holy Spirit.

---

[3] C. G. Patelos, ed., *The Orthodox Church in the Ecumenical Movement* (Geneva, 1978), p. 40.

[4] Ibid., p. 41.

But what is the nature of this fellowship? A fellowship is an association of people with common interests and goals, a partnership of equals committed to free and respectful dialogue, a community of friends engaged in living contact—talking, listening, learning, working and growing together in a spirit of mutual trust and love. The heart of this fellowship of churches is the confession of faith in the Lord Jesus Christ. To confess Christ is a response to what he has already done for us. He has loved us first. He has shed his blood on the cross for our forgiveness. He has risen from the dead to renew us by his divine power. He has sealed us with the Spirit of adoption making us sharers of the new covenant. We confess and receive him as Lord because he has already received us as co-heirs of his kingdom. Our common faith in Christ leads us to embrace one another as he has already embraced us. The words of Saint Paul to Jewish and Gentile Christians in the first century ring with awesome ecumenical relevance to the separated churches today: "Therefore, receive (*proslambanete*) one another just as (*kathos kai*) Christ has received (*proselabeto*) you to the glory of God"[5] (Rom 15.7).

Given the nature of our fellowship of churches, one might then ask to what degree has this fellowship matured in the ecumenical span of three generations? That is the spiritual challenge of BEM which must now be faced squarely because BEM is the result of an official charge of the member churches to the Faith and Order Commission working on their behalf. Let us seek to clear away all unnecessary confusions. BEM is presented to the churches for reception claiming neither exhaustiveness nor infallibility. BEM bears no ecclesial value except that which the member churches themselves may discover in one another through the process of reception. Reception at this early stage of the process by no means implies an official ecclesiastical act of an ultimate nature. The Vancouver Assembly clearly distinguished between, on the one hand, the "official response" of the churches "intended to initiate a process of study and communication" in each church as a body (rather than as individual or groups of individual theologians or church leaders), and, on the other hand, the long-range process of reception according to each church's own tradition which "will require much time and wide participation at various levels of the church."[6] Any official ecclesiastical act pertaining to BEM or aspects thereof might be taken only at the end of this spiritual pilgrimage which could take considerable time.

---

[5] See also Ulrich Kuhn, "Reception—An Imperative and an Opportunity," *Ecumenical Perspectives on Baptism, Eucharist and Ministry,* ed., Max Thurian (Geneva, 1983), p. 171.

[6] *Gathered for Life,* pp. 46-47.

Thus the question of the reception of BEM is a question of study, reflection, discussion, reaction and assimilation in the context of the spiritual and ecclesial freedom of the churches. The only authority of BEM is that it is not "their" text but "our" text—a common text of our fellowship. The truth of BEM is not truth deriving from some unquestioned source, or from any one Christian tradition, but truth which the churches themselves are willing to recognize as apostolic truth reflecting the faith of the Church of all ages under the assumption that the Holy Spirit is missing neither from any of the great moments of Christian history nor from any of the churches of the fellowship today. The process of reception involves what George Florovsky liked to call "ecumenism in time," not an all or nothing attitude of dialogical agreement in the light of the crystallized traditions of the churches today, but a circular process of listening to one another and of listening together to the common heritage of the apostolic faith.[7] A critical reaction to BEM is not merely saying yes or no to this or that part of BEM but above all entering by means of BEM into a deeper dialogue within the fellowship of churches, giving serious alternatives to the positions of BEM and being willing to exercise self-criticism toward renewal for the sake of the goal of unity. The cutting edge of BEM's witness is less at the point of any of its theological insights and tactical suggestions, all of which can be reformulated in the future as the churches see fit, but more at the point of testing the maturity of the churches as they seek to advance toward unity in the presence of Christ. The burden of BEM lies paradoxically not on itself but on the churches as they are willing or not to develop gradually a true consensus through the long "spiritual process of reception" involving "prayer and meditation, with penitence, thanksgiving, joy and hope."[8] The spiritual challenge of BEM for all churches is summed up by an invitation to "a genuine ecumenical conversion,"[9] which would serve as the indispensable, renewed spiritual basis of the fellowship of churches seeking unity in Christ.

Are the Orthodox Churches ready to meet the spiritual challenge of the Lima text? Are we spiritually ready to begin to respond constructively to theological and ecclesial issues of tremendous ecumenical implications? Are we ready to begin to contemplate future ecumenical commitments suggested by the BEM document, as for example the

---

[7] See Anton Houtepen, "Reception, Tradition, Communion," *Ecumenical Perspectives,* pp. 145-47.

[8] *Gathered for Life,* pp. 47-48.

[9] Max Thurian and Günther Gassmann, "The Faith and Order Document on Baptism, Eucharist and Ministry," *Information: Faith and Order,* February 1985, p. 2.

mutual recognition of sacraments, which are of the greatest magnitude for the unity of the divided churches? To begin to deal seriously with these issues is above all a spiritual matter requiring spiritual readiness! By spiritual readiness I mean being alive to the presence of the Spirit, "not taught by human wisdom but taught by the Spirit" (1 Cor 2.13), and interpreting truths with "the mind of Christ" (1 Cor 2.16). To answer these questions yes or no would be presumptuous and unhelpful. Most important is the fact that the Lima text is a concrete ecumenical challenge calling the Orthodox to discern our own spiritual readiness by prayer, study, reflection and self-criticism in order that the Spirit of God may lead us to witness to the fulness of faith and life in Christ. Nicholas Lossky has succinctly described what the spiritual challenge of BEM means for the Orthodox in the first place by using the word *metanoia*/repentance, defining it as a permanent attitude of submission of the human will to the divine. The BEM document forcefully reminds the Orthodox Church, so Lossky puts it, of its vocation of permanent conversion to Orthodoxy truly understood as the fulness of the life in Christ.[10] Authenticity in the fulness of the life in Christ is the indispensable convincing base for any other theological or ecclesial claims within an ecumenical fellowship.

One specific way in which the Orthodox ecumenical commitment will be tested is by the Orthodox readiness to use the Lima text as a study text at various levels and among various groupings in the life of the Church. Reflecting decades of ecumenical experience the BEM document clearly recognizes that the weight of church unity must rest not on a theological "convergence" by theologians and church representatives alone, but on a true "consensus" developed among all the people of God as well, understood as "that experience of life and articulation of faith necessary to realize and maintain the Church's visible unity."[11] We must admit that the Orthodox record in this respect is not at all encouraging. Ecumenical involvement has engaged: primarily theologians and hierarchs representing the Orthodox Churches in ecumenical meetings in Geneva or elsewhere; to some degree other Orthodox theologians and hierarchs back home; a few lay persons interested in theology and ecumenical relations; and finally and least of all (in some cases perhaps not at all), the Orthodox faithful. The reasons for this are many, among them administrative and spiritual inertia, and deep questions about the ecumenical movement which have

---

[10]Nicholas Lossky, "A quelle 'metanoia' le texte de Lima appele-t-il l'Eglise Orthodoxe?" *Unité des Chrétiens,* No. 57, January 1985, p. 23.

[11]*Baptism, Eucharist and Ministry: Faith and Order Paper No. 111* (Geneva, 1982). p. ix.

much greater force back home than in ecumenical meetings. But the fact remains that, as in the case of other churches, we face an enormous process of communication, education and motivation.[12] Some Orthodox theological schools have already begun to use the BEM document as a text in appropriate courses. The Orthodox ecumenical commitment will surely appear formal and superficial unless the Orthodox Churches initiate and monitor identifiable ways of ecumenical education at all levels of church life, involving bishops, theologians, lay leaders, teachers, local congregations and even children in their catechetical schools, as the broader context of the reception of BEM. Given the hierarchical nature of the Orthodox Churches, the bishops of our churches must involve ecumenically all their people in appropriate ways, not only for strategic reasons, but also because the truth of all episcopal and ecclesial commitments must ultimately be accepted by the living experience and the conscience of the people of God.[13]

Another way in which the BEM document will test the spiritual maturity and the ecumenical commitment of the Orthodox Churches will be in our willingness to review and correct actual practices which do not reflect the fulness of faith and life in Christ. One of the key stipulations of the presentation of BEM to the churches by Faith and Order is "the guidance your church can take from this text for its worship, educational, ethical, and spiritual life and witness."[14] BEM is not only an excellent educational text on such matters as the meaning of baptism, the social implications of the eucharist, the spirit of church leadership and many others, but BEM also challenges the churches to deal with lax or even erroneous practices and attitudes perpetuated by uncritical tradition. An early report on BEM by the Orthodox Theological Society in America,[15] which is both positive and reserved in spirit, candidly points out several examples of such practices in the Orthodox Churches. One example is what BEM calls indiscriminate infant baptism, that is, baptism without effective nurturing of parents and baptized children to mature commitment to Christ. The Orthodox report from the United States tersely admits: "This criticism is valid."[16] It goes on to state that "in some practices and attitudes we

---

[12]See also Jeffrey Gros, "Baptism, Eucharist and Ministry," *One World,* 103 (March 1985) 14.

[13]See Kallistos Ware, "The Ecumenical Councils and the Conscience of the Church," *Kanon: Jahrbuch der Gesellschaft für das Recht der Ostkirchen* (Vienna, 1974), 2, especially pp. 22ff.

[14]*Baptism, Eucharist and Ministry,* p. x.

[15]"A Report on *Baptism, Eucharist and Ministry,*" *The Greek Orthodox Theological Review,* 29 (1984) 401-18.

[16]Ibid., p. 406.

Orthodox have fallen short of providing [an] 'environment of witness and service' (BEM phraseology), and that we must develop a baptismal catechesis in the life of the Church, especially for parents and sponsors, as a basis for effective Christian nurturing of those who are baptized as infants.''[17] Other examples cited by the same report include passive formalism in worship, an individualistic approach to Holy Communion, the diminishment of the diaconate including the extinction of the office of deaconess, and autocratic clerical authority, all of which cannot stand comfortably under the searching light of BEM seeking to witness to the fulness of the apostolic life.

Thus the spiritual challenge of BEM at its deepest level provides an opportunity for the Orthodox Churches to embark upon a deliberate course of self-renewal, led by the bishops, and consciously aiming at a recovery of the fulness of *orthopraxia,* as well as *orthodoxia.* Otherwise the arduous ecumenical efforts of the Orthodox Churches will not yield abundant fruit to the glory of Christ. The truth of the Orthodox witness, as hinted above, is to be convincingly conveyed not only through symposia, theological literature, and ecumenical encounters, but also through evidence of new life in Christ, sacrificial service to the needy in the world, and genuine Christian fellowship so that others may see and be persuaded by, and not merely told about, the quality of Orthodox faith and life. BEM, as has been stated, has to do with life, and not only with theological agreements or ecclesiastical arrangements. Integral to the reception process of BEM is a process of spiritual renewal within the churches. Giving evidence of the lively presence of the Spirit among us, such renewal would also establish the necessary groundwork for engagement with the difficult theological and ecclesial issues that we face.

Theological Challenge

In the report "Taking Steps Toward Unity" the Vancouver Assembly (1983) proclaimed that *"what* the churches are asked to receive in this text [BEM] is not simply a document, but *in* this document the apostolic faith from which it comes, and to which it bears witness" (emphasis is the report's).[18] These weighty words sum up the theological challenge of the Lima text for all the churches: to work toward unity by arriving at a common understanding of the central sacraments of ecclesial life, namely, baptism, eucharist and ordained ministry, on the basis of the *apostolic faith.* The BEM document itself

---

[17]Ibid., p. 407. See also Thomas Hopko, "The Lima Statement and the Orthodox," *The Search for Visible Unity,* ed. Jeffrey Gros (New York, 1984), especially pp. 60-63, where Hopko writes about BEM's "judgment on the Orthodox."

[18]*Gathered for Life,* p. 48.

appeals to the apostolic faith, the apostolic tradition, and the apostolic ministry. BEM *is* a theological document but does not stand alone in the quest of unity. The churches agreed in Vancouver that a convincing witnessing unity would bear at least three marks not yet fully shared by the divided churches:[19]

1) reception of BEM looking to mutual recognition of baptism, eucharist and ministry;

2) a common understanding of the apostolic faith, with special attention to the Nicene Creed, through the current second great project of the Faith and Order Commission "Towards the Common Expression of the Apostolic Faith Today;"

3) and agreement on common ways of decision-making, ways of teaching authoritatively, and ways of corporate sharing and responsibility in the world.

Since Nairobi (1975) the above critical points have emerged as concrete steps which the churches can follow on the way to unity. Granted the seriousness of our will to unity, each church faces the burden of this question: if not these steps, then *what* steps?

As a theological challenge the BEM document does not seek to define the totality of the apostolic faith. It does not even claim to be an exhaustive theological treatment of the sacraments of baptism, eucharist and ministry. Rather its main purpose is to set down the essentials of the meaning, structure and place of these sacraments in ecclesial life in the light of the apostolic faith. A second important purpose is to lift up traditional points of disagreement, for example infant or adult baptism, and to *suggest* ways of overcoming them in the light of the apostolic faith and without illusions as to easy answers. Anyone who has seriously and honestly studied the New Testament and Church history must admit that in these two tasks the BEM document is on the whole eminently successful. BEM represents an amazing and unprecedented theological convergence which, given the spiritual will to unity as the call of Christ, can lead the churches toward a true consensus of faith and life in conjunction with the other desired marks of unity cited above. BEM is not chiseled on granite. Even essential points can be revised according to the mind of the churches. Indeed the whole document can, and most likely will, be reformulated in the long process of reception. But any church that is willing to attribute any serious theological and historical content to the word "apostolic" cannot evade

---

[19]Ibid., p. 19.

BEM's theological challenge: if not BEM, then *what*?"[20]

Thus the theological challenge of BEM converges on the meaning of the word "apostolic." One of the key ecumenical questions that has emerged from the work of Faith and Order is: what is the fulness of life in Christ according to the apostolic faith and order? The word "apostolic" is a critical reference to the common heritage of the churches. It would be both unwise and unhelpful to seek to define this word prematurely. It is up to the churches themselves, reflecting on the totality of the Christian ecclesial experience in history, to recognize each in its own life and practice, as well as in the life and practice of the other churches, what is truly apostolic.

However, this is not a vague, slippery word devoid of clear dimensions of meaning. For example, Montreal (1963) long ago set down the ecumenical principle of the centrality of the Gospel as inseparable from its reception by tradition: "Thus we can say that we exist as Christians by the tradition of the Gospel (the *paradosis* of the *kerygma*) testified in Scripture, transmitted in and by the Church through the power of the Holy Spirit" (*Montreal Report,* 2, 45). Similarly the Lima text appeals to the New Testament as well as to the writings of the Fathers (Baptism, 1). Although it does not name or quote any Fathers, its treatment of baptism, eucharist and ministry are anchored on the witness not only of the canonical Scriptures but also of the whole ancient Church. In fact some have expressed a wide opinion that BEM, because of its supposed heavy sacramental theology, primarily challenges those churches which resolutely hold to the supreme authority of Scripture and attach only secondary importance to sacramental life.[21] But does not the New Testament testify to the importance of baptism (e.g. Rom 6.1-11, despite 1 Cor 1.17) and the eucharist (1 Cor 10.14-22; 11.17-34)? Has not modern scholarship informed us about the fact that the early Church was above all a worshipping Church centered on the eucharist? On the other hand do we not also recognize the supremacy of Scripture in the Church Fathers? Have we not come more and more to acknowledge that apostolic succession must be defined as the continuity of the whole life of the Church bearing testimony to the lordship of Christ by the power of the Spirit? The word "apostolic" is meant precisely to set us on the course of discussing such issues and within such framework in order to arrive at an agreement about the unifying

---

[20]Tillard, p. 242, who writes these sobering words: BEM "is an arrow at the crossroads. Those churches who will not follow the sign will risk either arriving at a dead-end or discovering that they must return to the beginning of the ecumenical journey to see whether there exists another way."

[21]Lukas Vischer, "Unity in Faith," *Ecumenical Perspectives,* pp. 7-8.

essentials of the Christian faith, life and order.

What is BEM's theological challenge to the Orthodox Churches? It is interesting first to note that the early patriarchal encyclicals on the ecumenical movement actually counted on ecumenical cooperation and fellowship in practical matters and discouraged heavy involvement in doctrinal issues. For example the 1902 Patriarchal and Synodical Encyclical is doubtful about hope any of "union" because:

> The Western Church and the Church of the Protestants, . . . having taken their stand as on a base hardened by the passage of time, . . . seem quite disinclined to join on a road to union, such as is pointed out by the evangelical and historical truth; nor do they evince any readiness to do so, except on terms and bases on which the desired dogmatic unity and fellowship is unacceptable to us.[22]

The 1920 Patriarchal Encyclical, although replete with strong theological language about the proposed fellowship of churches, is content to suggest many ways of practical and friendly cooperation including "impartial and deeper historical study of doctrinal differences both by *seminaries* and in *books*" (emphasis is the writer's) but is eloquently silent about any face-to-face doctrinal discussions toward unity.[23] Even as late as 1952 another patriarchal encyclical clearly distinguishes between, on the one hand, "the principle aim of the World Council of Churches . . . the cooperation of the Churches on the plane of social and practical issues," and, on the other hand, "the 'Faith and Order' organization [which] still exists as a special Commission of the Council which is occupied exclusively with dogmatic questions."[24] The encyclical immediately goes on to warn:

> It is meet that any participation by the Orthodox Church in the discussions and operations of this Commission should be avoided, inasmuch as this Commission has for its aim the union (of Churches) by means of dogmatic discussions between delegates of Churches separated from one another by the deepest issues; this should be plainly and categorically stated to the Central Committee of the Council. But it is also necessary that our Orthodox Church should also inform the heterodox about the content of her faith . . . through books written for this special purpose.[25]

---

[22]*Orthodox Church in the Ecumenical Movement,* p. 30.

[23]Ibid., pp. 40-43.

[24]Ibid., p. 45.

[25]Ibid.

I offer the above references not to pursue the reasons behind the expressed Orthodox reluctance to discuss doctrinal issues, which reasons probably are in the main the perceived lack of any possibility of any success and the risk of impeding cooperation even on the practical plane, but in order to point out that a fellowship of churches *can* exist and be worthy of its name for the purpose of practical cooperation and service to the world in many and immensely important areas. The Orthodox did not necessarily have to join in the work of Faith and Order or they could have joined only as observers. Yet the underlying desire for unity, the predilection of many Orthodox to discuss theology, as well as changing perceptions about the possibilities of unity have led many Orthodox in the last decades to *insist* that the World Council place theology and issues of unity at the center of its agenda, as we all know. This is entirely consistent with the constitutional basis of the World Council, the Orthodox ecumenical commitment, as well as the spiritual responsibility implied by that commitment. The World Council has fulfilled the request of the Orthodox. But now, if the Orthodox Churches show reluctance in genuine engagement with BEM and other Faith and Order projects, they would seem to be contradicting their own expressed desires. Then the fellowship of churches would have a right to say to us: "We piped to you, and you did not dance; we wailed (about unity), and you did not mourn" (Mt 11.17)!

However, given the nature of the process of reception, the Orthodox Churches have no theological reason to hesitate in responding to the BEM document but rather they have reason to rejoice because of the opportunity of witnessing to the fulness of their faith and life in Christ. We should be eager in the spirit of Christian humility, and not in the spirit of triumphalism, to help the other churches of the fellowship to understand the full meaning of the word "apostolic." For example a discussion of the Orthodox understanding of sacrament as *mysterion,* which is grounded in the life of the community of faith, which requires a living faith by the participants, and centers on the action of the Holy Spirit rather than human formulae, would help in BEM's efforts to overcome the false dichotomy between word and sacrament and would help relieve Protestant fears of quasi-magical sacramentalism. The eucharist itself is a fervent prayer of the community of faith, celebrating and appropriating the very content of the Gospel through liturgical action, and looking to Christ as the true High Priest who makes himself present in the whole eucharistic event by the power of the Spirit.

Because as Orthodox we feel that we have maintained over the centuries a remarkable consensus in theology, spirituality, moral teaching and ecclesial life, we can welcome BEM's appeal to the witness of the apostolic tradition and seek to support it on a greater scale. But we will also be challenged in other ways by the BEM document, and especially by the specifics of what is essential to the apostolic tradition. While BEM strives to help the churches establish a theological coherence of faith and life, it also takes a strong position on behalf of the freedom of the churches regarding those things which are not absolutely essential to unity. Unity is not uniformity, so we have agreed. There is proper unity but there is also proper variety. Have not modern biblical and patristic studies shown to us an almost painful degree of development and variety in writings, forms of worship and practices in the ancient Church, a variety that could not be imagined by most theologians only a few generations ago? How the Orthodox react to the principle of variety when concretely applied, and how strongly we will support the effort to transcend the false dichotomies between Scripture and tradition, word and sacrament, clergy and laity, words of institution and epiklesis, and others, will partly depend on our willingness to absorb the results of contemporary biblical and patristic studies which are clearly presupposed by the Lima text.

One case in point is the long-standing controversy over infant and adult baptism (called ''believer's baptism by BEM with unfortunate connotations for baptized infants who would then seem to have no place in the community of faith). The ancient apostolic tradition witnesses to both practices! Although the practice of infant baptism eventually prevailed, the delay of baptism is also well known at least up to the fifth century. Granted that some of the great Fathers advised against it, and that infant baptism is desirable, but is it also absolutely required from the standpoint of Orthodox theology? Is it a theologically divisive issue? Another far more difficult case in point is that of the forms of the ordained ministry. BEM affirms the priestly, sacramental and constitutive character of the ordained ministry in ecclesial life. It also recommends the three-fold ordained ministry of bishop, presbyter and deacon as a welcome sign of unity but recognizes the variety of church order to which the New Testament and early patristic writings witness. *Episkope* is constitutive in the life of the Church but it can be exercised by means of different names and forms. Is the three-fold pattern absolute to unity? Must the ordained leader of a local church, who exercises the ministry of *episkope,* necessarily be called *episkopos*/bishop, rather than, let us say, *proestos*/president or even *poimen*/shepherd/ pastor? Would such differences in vocabulary be theologically divisive? These and other similar issues will have to be thoroughly examined and discussed during the period of the reception of BEM in the light of the best historical and theological scholarship. The Orthodox cannot assume *a priori* that, when the ancient Greek, Latin, Syriac, and Ethiopian Churches had different biblical canons without for that reason being

divided, every aspect of the apostolic tradition must be repeated in ecclesial life today. For the sake of obeying Christ's call, and helping
others also to obey it, not only unity but also legitimate variety must
be held as equally important.

Another area in which the Orthodox Churches are challenged by
BEM is that of the ethical and social implications of the sacraments
(e.g., see Baptism, 10; Eucharist, 20,25; Ministry, 4,34). Vancouver
(1983) also insisted that concern about unity and sacraments cannot
be separated from concern about peace, justice, working against racism,
fighting hunger and the like. The Lima text "has underlined for us that
baptism, eucharist and ministry are healing and uniting signs of a
Church living and working for a renewed and reconciled
humankind."[26] A truly eucharistic life-style includes "a constant
challenge in the search for appropriate relationships in social, economic
and political life" (BEM, Eucharist, 20). These are strong words for
the Orthodox who are conditioned by their own historical and cultural
experience. But Orthodox ecumenical theologians have clearly acknowledged as integral to their own tradition the truth that the Church
is the active supporter and defender of suffering humanity in any conditions of suffering on behalf of a loving God.[27] It remains a challenge
for the Orthodox Churches to apply this truth in appropriate ways according to their particular situations. The Orthodox Churches have
every reason to lift up not only the social ethical, but also the personal
ethical, implications of the sacraments. Is there to be a new dichotomy
between social and personal ethics? Too long Orthodox theologians have
been ecumenically silent about grave issues pertaining to personal
morality, sexuality and indiscriminate abortion on demand.[28] On the
way to unity—are we as Orthodox to count the settling of the exact
vocabulary of the ordained ministries as more important to God than
the resolution of a grave moral problem costing tens of millions of un-
born lives annually? Or, according to Orthodox theology, is unity in
Christ and the sharing of a common eucharistic table possible among
those who hold to diametrically opposite ethical values?

A final theological challenge to the Orthodox Churches arises not
from the contents of the BEM document but from what the reception
of BEM might mean for the Protestant Churches, especially those deeply
impacted by the spirit modern liberalism. Underneath the growing

---

[26]*Gathered for Life,* p. 49.

[27]See especially *Martyria/Mission: The Witness of the Orthodox Churches Today,* ed.
Ion Bria (Geneva, 1980).

[28]This writer somewhat naively tried to raise this issue on the floor of the Vancouver
Assembly as one worthy of study, and later was privately supported by a few Protestant
representatives and Roman Catholic observers, but to no avail.

ecumenical trust a deep anxiety smolders among the Orthodox, an anxiety reflecting the doctrinal hesitations of the patriarchal encyclicals quoted above, that the Protestant world will not accept and will not be bound by any doctrinal agreements. Thomas Hopko expresses this Orthodox anxiety when he speaks about worries that "each church will interpret BEM in its own way," that "some churches will not treat [BEM] at all seriously because they consider the issues . . . secondary and unimportant," that the Protestant churches "are no longer capable of acting authoritatively as churches," and that "others may treat the whole effort with indifference, cynicism, or outright contempt."[29] These fears are not at all unfounded. Even Protestant ecumenical figures not infrequently make statements which are deeply disquieting to Orthodox doctrinal sensitivities. For example, after the celebration of the Lima Liturgy in Vancouver, in which the Orthodox did not receive Holy Communion for known serious theological reasons, a prominent Protestant ecumenical figure was quoted by the Assembly *Canvas* as saying: "At last, praise God, we can accept together the bread and wine, the body and blood, without those dreadful hangups we've had for so long." This ecumenical figure was obviously speaking about Protestants, but describing theological differences not permitting the sharing of the cup as "dreadful hangups" was not at all reassuring to Orthodox about Protestant seriousness over doctrinal issues. The seeming inertia of the Orthodox Churches in responding to BEM and initiating a process of reception among the Orthodox people is in part preconditioned by this sense of helplessness regarding the value of theological agreements in the face of Protestant freedom of opinion. In the ecumenical journey the Orthodox are likely both to appreciate and to engage more and more in practical ecumenism . . . but can the mainline Protestants ever do the same in doctrinal ecumenism on the basis of classic biblical and patristic categories of faith and life? One can be sure that the Orthodox in the coming years will be watching Protestant reactions not only to BEM but also, and perhaps with greater interest, the parallel project of Faith and Order "Towards the Common Expression of the Apostolic Faith Today."

The Ecclesiological Challenge

The ecclesiological challenge is equally sensitive and difficult. BEM's ultimate purpose is the mutual recognition of sacraments by the churches. Even now BEM gently encourages churches "to attain a greater measure of eucharistic communion" (BEM, Eucharist 33). Although it speaks about "the Church," "the apostolic Church," and

---

[29]Hopko, pp. 56-57.

"the Church of every time and place," the Lima text does not explicitly deal with the doctrine of the Church. Therefore it leaves itself open to the criticism that the sacraments in BEM seem to be unrelated to one another and seem somehow to stand in mid-air. One Orthodox theologian expressed his concern about the precedence of the Church with this oral declaration in Vancouver: "Not where *sacraments* are, there also is the Church, but rather where the *Church* is, there also are sacraments."

But it would be entirely unfair to expect BEM to begin with the ecclesiological problem. This problem can be addressed directly, at any rate for the Orthodox, only when the process of the reception of BEM matures and when the eventual process of reception of a common expression of faith is also completed. A common confession of faith is a prerequisite to the full reception of BEM and to agreement on any other particular issues of ecclesiological nature. Meanwhile we must rest on the principle that the only doctrinal criterion for joining the World Council of Churches is its trinitarian basis. Toronto (1950) affirmed that membership does not imply surrender of a church's ecclesiology, nor acceptance of that of another. The World Council, as it often repeats to minimize confusion on this matter, has no ecclesial status or ecclesial authority of its own.

But of course that is not the whole story. A deep ecclesiological tension exists in the World Council of Churches, and is inevitably carried by BEM as a document of the World Council. This tension, which is felt most sharply by the Orthodox Churches, is in part intrinsic to the ecumenical venture and will not be resolved until the ecumenical journey reaches its goal. But the tension can be discussed, clarified and appropriately treated so as to remain a creative tension prompting the churches toward unity rather than a negative one generating unnecessary frustration. This tension is between, on the one hand, the *implied* ecclesiology of the World Council of Churches and BEM which is so loud, and, on the other hand, the *explicit* ecclesiology of the Orthodox Churches constituting the one, holy, catholic and apostolic Church which is so silent in the ecumenical arena. The fruits of this tension are misunderstanding and impatience for many Protestants and frustration and disillusionment for many Orthodox. Whatever the growing trust among ecumenical theologians and church representatives, the Orthodox Churches as churches will not be able to take the World Council seriously as *their* Council and BEM as *their* document, until the unnecessary and negative side of this tension is relieved, which is a responsibility of both the Orthodox Churches and the Council. Because this ecclesiological problem is one of the crucial factors determining the reception of BEM by the Orthodox Churches, it is necessary to deal with it in the last section of this paper.

The entire family of canonical Orthodox Churches has not slackened but rather increased in recent years its ecumenical commitment to the quest for Christian unity through participation in the World Council of Churches and in bilateral dialogues. One might venture to say that Orthodox ecumenical involvement will continue on a more effective basis as Orthodox ecumenical participation matures and as the Orthodox people, clergy and laity, are appropriately informed about the true bases and goals of Orthodox ecumenism in all its forms. The Orthodox Churches owe an immense gratitude in particular to the World Council of Churches not only for innumerable spiritual, educational and material benefits but also for the Council's conscious or unconscious help in bringing the Orthodox Churches into the world context of the twentieth century as living rather than ancient churches. Not least of all the World Council has also helped in generating greater interaction among the Orthodox Churches themselves in our century. Notwithstanding these and many other benefits, the Orthodox Churches are deeply committed to the World Council of Churches for spiritual and theological reasons: 1) the call to fulfill Christ's will for unity; 2) the imperative of witnessing to the faith and order of the one, holy, catholic and apostolic Church; and 3) the urgent mandate of Christian cooperation in practical matters, common witness and service to the world. Whatever the obstacles, the Orthodox Churches cannot cease ecumenical engagement and remain true to their own mission in the world. Christ requires it. The very nature of the Church requires it. Christian love and truth require it. The needs of the world require it.

And yet, as we know, the Orthodox Churches have been experiencing an ecclesiological "discomfort" of considerable magnitude within the World Council of Churches (as have other churches for their own reasons). On a corporate level this sense of discomfort, at times perhaps suffocation, broke out through *The Sofia Consultation,*[30] an agressive, even strident voicing of Orthodox feelings about the nature of Orthodox involvement in the World Council of Churches. Whatever the right or wrong claims of *The Sofia Consultation,* the discomfort must be effectively addressed. It was again felt in Vancouver (1983) on several occasions, especially when an issue of clear Orthodox interest was raised on the Assembly floor and unwisely brought to a vote, and then of course the Orthodox were simply overwhelmed by the Protestant majority. This was not merely defeat: this was humiliation, unintended and momentary as it was. A similar painful moment on a personal level,

---

[30]*The Sofia Consultation: Orthodox Involvement in the World Council of Churches,* ed. Todor Sabev (Geneva, 1982).

if the writer is allowed a brief reference to his personal experience in Vancouver, occurred during the Lima Eucharist which was otherwise for him an impressive and inspiring event. At the time of Holy Communion, he was compelled, because the rows of chairs were so close together, to follow the immediate participants, and then to come before one of the many Communion Cups along the aisles, and thus having to *reject the Cup* according to his conscience—a personal moment of unprecedented pain and humiliation. Of course this "judgment" of conscience by compulsion was unintended but apparently those responsible for the arrangement of the reception of Holy Communion, although the worship committee included Orthodox, forgot all the hundreds of Orthodox Christians present and their own deep sensitivities pertaining to Holy Communion. In their enthusiasm the Protestants in many ways wanted to involve the Orthodox in the celebration of the Lima Eucharist without, of course, compelling them to receive Holy Communion. While some Orthodox did not seem to mind participating officially in the service, of course not taking Holy Communion, others were deeply disquieted by it and viewed the Protestant warm hospitality in this case as an expression of an embrace of overbearing love.

I mention all of the above with the conviction that, as a matter of sensitive ecumenical policy and courtesy, such things should not occur —and that includes some of the words and part of the spirit of *The Sofia Consultation,* too. My point is that the unnecessary and unhelpful part of the tension can be relieved only by finding a sensitive balance in the relationship between the Orthodox Churches and the World Council without compromising the integrity and the rights of either. When I speak of balance I mean that the Orthodox Churches are within the Council but also outside of the Council constituting one Orthodox Church in a unique way not applicable to other member churches. The memorandum from the Ecumenical Patriarchate in *The Sofia Consultation* clearly states: "The Orthodox Church is not the same as its other member churches and that local Orthodox Churches cannot be considered and treated simply as 'ecclesiastical bodies.' "[31] Without such a balance the Orthodox Churches will continue to feel at best as "guests" within the massive fellowship of churches and at worst as "co-opted" in various ways by it. It is not a question of dominance and control but a question of Christian love and freedom on both sides for the sake of authentic ecumenical engagement. The finding of this balance is the responsibility not only of the World Council but of the Orthodox Churches themselves truly working together as one Orthodox Church.

I want to make clear that I am not suggesting that the basic problem

---

[31]Ibid., p. 69.

is simply administrative. It is rather ecclesiological. The overwhelming tone, literature and vision of the World Council as a "conciliar fellowship" both presupposes and seeks to give practical expression to a Protestant ecclesiology, one that simultaneously holds to the historical divisions and also the spiritual unity of all the Christian churches. Since all churches somehow share an essential unity in Christ, what remains is to *manifest this unity* more fully and visibly through theological agreement, practical cooperation, common witness and a consensus of faith and life among the churches that would lead to the desired common cup. Some of these ideas, at least in limited ways, are correct from the perspective of Orthodox theology because all the churches confess the Triune God and seek sincerely to serve him in spirit and truth. We must also recognize the right of Protestant member churches to voice such an ecclesiology within the World Council and to act with one another in ways that are appropriate to this ecclesiology. But the World Council *as a council* must not allow—and this is the crux of the problem— Protestant ecclesiology to dominate its spirit and documents, especially significant documents such as BEM, because as a matter of course and to an inverse degree the ecclesial witness of the Orthodox Churches being the one, holy, catholic and apostolic Church is silenced.[32] Whether implicitly or explicitly both types of ecclesiology must be given attention and must be brought into positive dialogue in appropriate ways especially in key documents.

A subtle but powerful indication of the implicit dominance of Protestant ecclesiology, to give another example, may be discerned in the more or less official World Council terminology which applies the expression "the Church" (with capital "C") to the assumed larger reality of the invisible Church somehow already existing and to be more fully manifested in the future, while the expression "the churches" (with small "c") is applied to the divided Christian bodies, including the Orthodox Churches. That these expressions are more than stylistic matters is indicated by another equally subtle but powerful tendency in ecumenical language to refer to the Orthodox reality by means of the plural "Orthodox churches" rather than the singular "Orthodox Church" with obvious, if unconscious implications. In other words Protestant ecclesiology is so deeply assumed and so overwhelmingly prevalent in the tone and literature of the World Council that to many Protestants, in many cases because of unfamiliarity pertaining to the historic position

---

[32]Thus in the context of responding to BEM the Orthodox Theological Society in America finds it necessary to explicate that "the Church of Christ, in its fulness, is not merely a spiritual reality reflected in a host of the Christian communities with differing confessions and liturgical practices. Rather, she is a concrete historical reality that we understand to be the Holy Orthodox Church," p. 401.

of the Orthodox Church, authentic Orthodox ecclesiological statements smack of "ecclesiological triumphalism," "theological imperialism," or a "theology of glory," unworthy of the Lord who washed his disciples' feet and offered himself on the cross for the life of the world. Thus in spite of the Toronto principle, and in spite of the clear principles of Orthodox ecumenism, the Orthodox Churches are placed by force of uncritical circumstances in a defensive position and our representatives are time and again pressured to surrender explicit expressions of their own ecclesiology by reason of the prevailing ecumenical dynamics.

Unfortunately we Orthodox representatives involved in the ecumenical movement not only have yielded to this pressure, undoubtedly not to risk raising extremely sensitive issues, but also have at times served as unwitting promoters of this assumed and prevalent ecclesiology. To give an example from a statement by Orthodox theologians drafted at the "Consultation on the Church's Struggle for Justice and Unity" in Crete (1975):

> . . . all should strive in their churches [note small "c"] and traditions to deepen the fulness of the apostolic faith embodied in a fully ecclesial life . . . No church is therefore required to lose its distinctive character . . . The unity of the Church [note capital "C"] should be understood as common participation in the true Tradition . . . given by Christ . . . a unity which increases . . . a dynamic process . . . towards the perfect unity which will only be revealed at the end of time . . .[33]

The above statement is tantalizingly ambiguous confusing two kinds of unity by means of theological "ecumenese." It is true insofar as a *spiritual unity* of hearts and minds is concerned, a unity that can wane and wax, a unity that should be pursued among the Orthodox themselves. But it is not true insofar as the *ecclesial unity* of the one, holy, catholic and apostolic Church is concerned, identified by objective doctrinal, sacramental and canonical boundaries, whatever the spiritual shortcomings of its diverse members.

Still more unfortunate are occasional liturgical instances in which Orthodox hierarchs and theologians seem to cross over proper guidelines of ecumenical worship. Yes, we are committed to ecumenical prayer

---

[33]*Orthodox Church in the Ecumenical Movement,* p. 117. The above words are quoted from several paragraphs in the original. For another example of ecumenical ecclesiological ecumenese hesitating to identify the Orthodox Church as the one, holy, catholic and apostolic Church, see the Damascus Statement in preparation for the Vancouver Assembly (1983) in *Jesus Christ—the Life of the World,* ed. Ion Bria (Geneva, 1982) pp. 12-14.

and ecumenical prayer services. Prayer gives us spiritual unity by the grace of God. Prayer is essential to our quest for ecclesial unity. But what happened in Vancouver at the Lima Eucharist, so at least this writer would strongly counsel, should not again occur. At the Lima Eucharist Orthodox hierarchs and priests officially participated in the great liturgical entrance, proceeded up into the area of liturgical action, recited liturgical prayers, read biblical readings, and then stepped down from that area in order not to take part in the eucharist proper and, of course, not to receive Holy Communion. But can the eucharist be divided in that fashion? Does not BEM itself instruct us that "the whole action of the eucharist has an 'epikletic' character" (BEM, Eucharist, 16)? Is not the whole eucharist one sacramental event? Did not participation in the Lima Eucharist blur, where it should have made clear by means of painful regrets, authentic witness to Orthodox ecclesiology on the part of the Orthodox themselves? To this writer, the act of "stepping down" at a crucial point in the Lima Eucharist seemed not only superficial but actually more offensive than official nonparticipation would have been. I also had mixed feelings about the Orthodox Liturgy as an ecumenical event, which was impressively celebrated amidst a throng of Protestants and Orthodox. Not only were the Orthodox cast in the role of being "observed" by the Protestants, but also some Protestants were pained and offended by not being able to receive Holy Communion. For all these reasons, I do not think that it is helpful to celebrate eucharists in such ecumenical contexts where some would receive Communion and others would not.

Therefore the Toronto statement and other basic ecumenical principles now and then clarified by the World Council do not of themselves relieve the ecclesiological confusion as far as the Orthodox are concerned, although the frequent articulation of these basic principles is a necessary reminder about the true nature of the World Council and the Orthodox Church. In addition careful steps must be taken in order to clear up this ecclesiological confusion which fundamentally weakens the Orthodox ecumenical involvement by blurring the authenticity of the Orthodox witness. The Orthodox Churches have sufficiently matured in the ways of ecumenism within the World Council to pursue these steps in a proper spirit and with proper leadership, steps which may initially appear challenging to the fellowship of churches but will in the long run strengthen it by means of genuine theological dialogue on the basis of the true positions of the member churches. What are, then, some of these steps?

The first step, as many Orthodox theologians have already suggested, is a more essential qualitative and quantitative participation in the work of the World Council, i.e., an actualization of the Orthodox presence applying across the board and involving administration, finances, policies, commissions and programs. The twenty-three percent quota system for Orthodox representation is not of itself the answer, and Orthodox insistence on it would seem to make us both tiresome and impinging on the rights of other churches. A key structural answer is needed by which the Orthodox Churches can work as one Orthodox Church with respect to the World Council, without necessarily ceasing individual membership. Just because all the Orthodox Churches entered into the World Council individually, the future nature of their involvement and membership does not have to remain unchanged. Perhaps the establishment of a Pan-Orthodox Ecumenical Commission with a permanent office at the Patriarchal Orthodox Center in Geneva, coordinating Orthodox ecumenical priorities and strategies, could be a first move toward finding the right answer *within* the World Council. Perhaps a balanced answer may not be found until the Roman Catholic Church itself is engaged in this discussion in the hope of also joining the World Council. In any case it is imperative that the Orthodox Churches, along with the right of their individual membership in the World Council, should find ways of representing themselves and acting as one Orthodox Church within the Council, if their ecclesiological witness is to bear weight.

A second step is a more clear explication of Orthodox ecclesiology in an ecumenical context which would do justice both to authentic Orthodox ecclesiology and to the deep Orthodox commitment to contemporary ecumenism renouncing superficial triumphalism and traditional polemics. This task belongs primarily to Orthodox leaders and theologians themselves. Much has already been done in the area of eucharistic ecclesiology. Now there is a need for a clear articulation of the value of *canonical unity* as a sign of ecclesial unity from an Orthodox perspective. The ecclesial unity of the one, holy, catholic and apostolic Church has never been lost but endures in the ongoing history of the family of canonical Orthodox Churches. Orthodox ecclesiology holds to the principle that ecclesial unity can neither be historically existent nor theologically conceived except as a full communion of a family of churches united doctrinally, sacramentally and *canonically*. The reading of the diptychs is not merely a formal but rather an essential sign of ecclesial unity. Canonicity is not only a legal but also theological notion expressing a mutual sharing of the catholicity of the Church as an ongoing historical reality. To ignore or be silent about the fact that the one, holy, catholic and apostolic Church has a street address dismays the Orthodox, especially the Orthodox back home, and serves no purpose as far as an ultimate solution to the ecclesiological problem of the World Council of Churches is concerned.

A third step is the involvement of a more clear and properly balanced ecclesiological phraseology in all World Council affairs and documents in order to maintain the integrity of Orthodox ecclesiology while neither slighting other member churches nor suggesting necessary compliance by them to Orthodox ecclesiological principles, unless of course they become freely and inwardly convinced of the truth of these principles. The quality and timing of Orthodox initiatives in this regard are, to be sure, extremely sensitive matters. Superficial triumphalism is entirely out of bounds, one might even say, reprehensible to a true ecumenical spirit. The Christian principles of love and freedom do not allow even hints of demands of capitulation on any points but only genuine dialogue in mutual trust and respect with a prayerful seeking to persuade each other openly and without defensive attitudes about the truth of the distinctive positions of the member churches—in order that Christ himself may convert us to the one Truth.

But the ecclesiological problem cannot be silenced or confused without doing a disservice to true ecumenism within the World Council or other councils of churches throughout the world. How the ecclesiological problem is to be elucidated is the responsibility of all the member churches. The Orthodox should not again request the issuance of separate statements but rather seek a clearer ecclesiological phraseology and economically formulated expression of their distinctive ecclesiological and doctrinal views on key issues whenever these are treated in ecumenical documents. At the same time it should be made clear that the Orthodox are not in the World Council only to witness to the Orthodox faith but also to share in a common witness and to learn from other Christians as well. Thus, while the dynamic process of spiritual unity among the member churches toward a more perfect unity may be recognized, and while the truth that the Orthodox Churches, too, need to live the fulness of the apostolic life by ongoing spiritual renewal may also be affirmed, nevertheless the ecclesial self-understanding of the Orthodox Church that it is the one, holy, catholic and apostolic Church need not be held under a bushel but rather be humbly proclaimed as part of an ecumenism of truth in love. Too, this claim is a terrible burden on the family of Orthodox Churches to manifest convincingly their ecclesial unity in their mutual relations and common witness.

A fourth and final step in dealing with the ecclesiological problem is a courageous exploration on the part of the Orthodox pertaining to the ecclesial status not of the World Council as a Council, but of the member churches, i.e., an effort to articulate in what positive sense, wherever possible, a member church possesses ecclesial reality no matter how provisional or incomplete that reality is. That the Orthodox

Church is the one, holy, catholic and apostolic Church does not at imply that other Christian churches are nothing. Is acceptance of the trinitarian basis of the World Council an ecclesial sign in terms of doctrine? Is acceptance of the Lima text an ecclesial sign in terms of the sacraments? Are living faith in Christ, vigorous worship and true preaching of the Gospel by the power of the Spirit ecclesial signs? Are selfless love, effective mission and sacrificial service to the world in the name of Christ ecclesial signs? Yes, by all means!

Traditionally the Orthodox Churches have not developed positive means of relating to other Christian bodies but rather have looked upon them in the categories of schism and heresy which could be healed only by repentance and return to the Orthodox Church. But these categories are wholly inappropriate in the context of the World Council of Churches involving historic Protestant Churches with centuries of tradition, teaching and witness, and which were never related to the Orthodox Church. Wholesale renunciation of their tradition and massive capitulation to contemporary Orthodoxy would be as unrealistic as it would be wrong. The Orthodox need to realize that this avenue to Christian unity is closed. Rather the Orthodox need to accept the necessity of a long period of growth in a spiritual unity of hearts and minds through authentic dialogue and cooperation, and of witnessing to the key signs of the fulness of apostolic faith and order, while fervently praying for a day when by God's grace other churches may become ready to consider and to discuss communion with the family of Orthodox Churches without surrendering their autonomy. Meanwhile the Orthodox leaders and theologians need gradually to express themselves on the ecclesial status of other churches in the spirit of Vatican II or at least on the fundamental signs of ecclesial reality in any separated church, if the Orthodox ecumenical commitment is to have deep value, and if the Orthodox witness to the fulness of the apostolic faith, life and order is to carry ringing conviction.

Reception of the BEM Document in the Orthodox Tradition: A Response to the Paper of Theodore Stylianopoulos

K. M. GEORGE

I MUST BEGIN by expressing my unreserved appreciation for what Father Stylianopoulos has presented to us. He has articulated his reflections on a double front. On the one hand he has clarified his critical and positive approach to the BEM document from the Orthodox perspective in a very creative manner. This is done in the spirit that "it is not their text, but our text—a common text of our fellowship." On the other hand he has critically examined the Orthodox position from the perspective of the BEM document bringing out the spiritual, theological, and ecclesiological challenges and possibilities. He has also highlighted the commitment of the ecumenical movement in general and that of the Faith and Order Commission in particular to the one, holy, catholic and apostolic tradition and the reciprocal commitment of the Orthodox churches to the world fellowship of Christians. The BEM document seems to be understood by Father Stylianopoulos as an initial test of this mutual commitment. We must be immensely grateful for his reflections.

As an Indian Orthodox Christian, the Indian religious-philosophical tradition and the Eastern Christian tradition are part of my heritage. The Indian religious tradition does not have any notion of blasphemy or heresy as we see in Judaism or Christianity. People with widely varying views are accommodated within the mainstream of Hindu religion. It is legitimate for a person to say: "I am Brahman (God)" without being blasphemous. In fact it is the ultimate level of spiritual realization when the human and the divine are no longer distinguished, but experienced as one single reality. The major Indian philosophical traditions do not know of any ultimate distinction between the Creator and the creature. A person who perceives only distinction, without realizing the non-difference between his self and the ultimate Self is in the state of *maya* (illusion) or *avidya* (ignorance). Even the so-called atheistic strands of thought are accommodated within the religious tradition. An atheistic position need not necessarily be a materialistic one. Denying God or being silent about God may sometimes be the expression of the highest spiritual experience as in the case of Buddha. An enlightened soul knows that there is *no God* apart from his realized self.

Now, the change from darkness to light, from ignorance to true knowledge does not occur as a sudden transition. It is a gradual process necessitating much askesis, spiritual, mental and physical discipline. In this process of spiritual enlightenment one is not preoccupied with doctrinal questions of purely intellectual-verbal categories. One discerns only different levels of understanding and different degrees in the intensity of experience. Spiritual life is understood as a gradual growth from inferior levels to superior levels of understanding and self-realization.

Without subscribing to any of these religious-philosophical ideas, one can find here some striking parallels with the patristic thought which is constitutive of the Eastern Christian Tradition.

1. In the Tradition of the Christian East, the primary concern is not with propositional orthodoxy. In spite of the great significance of creeds and conciliar decrees in the life of the Church, it is understood that intellectual assent to a credal proposition does not in itself constitute right belief. There is a great reluctance on the part of the Church to proliferate creeds, confessions and statements of faith. Fathers like Saint Basil of Caesarea, Saint Gregory the Theologian, and Saint Gregory of Nyssa took great pains to establish the Orthodox principle that logically coherent, rationally clear and scripturally argued propositions about God do not necessarily constitute genuine *theologia,* but they might run the risk of becoming pure *technologia* leading to vain talk about God and to a war of words. The integral and experiential relation between talking about God (*theologein*) and "becoming God (*theon genesthai*)," and that between dogma and doxa, are held very high by the Church over against all excessive concern with propositional orthodoxy.

2. The patristic tradition recognizes that God's self-revelation in human history has been a gradual process respecting the freedom of human beings. The whole human history is understood as a stage of God's subtle, loving, persuasive—not compelling—act of raising

humanity to higher and higher levels of spiritual receptivity. Saint Gregory of Nazianos, in his theological orations tells us that theology or knowledge of the Holy Trinity develops by gradual additions. The Father makes himself known fully in the Old Testament period while the Son and the Holy Spirit are only adumbrated. In the New Testament period, God the Son is fully revealed while the fulness of the Holy Spirit is only promised. After the Pentecost, the person and power of the Holy Spirit are fully manifested. The divine economy is based on the recognition that there are various levels of spiritual perception and capacity for reception and that higher levels of receptivity are attained only gradually, in freedom and through sustained mutual interaction between God and humanity. If we are involved in this experiential process of growth, we cannot think of the life of the Church primarily in terms of schisms or heresies. Although the fathers vehemently criticized all malicious and deliberate distortions of faith, they also understood that it is our common task and responsibility to sharpen and focus the various levels of spiritual sensitivity within the community in the direction of the Good, to correct each other, to carry each other's burdens and to sustain the feeble in faith by closely integrating them to the community of faith.

I mentioned these two aspects of Orthodox understanding because they might be helpful in evaluating the BEM document in the process of reception, and also understanding what Father Stylianopoulos has stated in his paper with great discernment and balance. Referring to my first comment about propositional orthodoxy and speaking in a rather reductionist manner, I would say that the BEM document is a multiple set of theological propositions shaped by a group or group of theologians over the years. Over half a century ago when Faith and Order discussions started culminating in the production of the present document, there was no effective Orthodox and Roman Catholic involvement or input. The major assumption and motivation of the Faith and Order movement then was that a doctrinal agreement among several Protestant denominations could be brought about through commonly agreed theological statements, and thereby unity of these churches could be achieved. Gradually Orthodox and Roman Catholic Churches came in to share this assumption and ideal. There is no need to question this basic goal, because it is the goal of unity which is constitutive of the ecumenical movement to which world Christianity is committed. But methodologically, if there is any lingering of the idea that commonly agreed, neatly defined theological propositions are the major instrument of unity, that should be of serious concern to us.

Father Theodore makes it very clear that this "reception" of the BEM document at this stage does not "signify that ecclesial process through which the Orthodox Church has received the authoritative decrees of Ecumenical Synods. . . . " But *ultimately* is it not the same ecclesial process the Churches are committed to by consenting to consider the question of reception? Are we not entering already the inarticulate but initial stages of that process? When that process matures it will not be the BEM document as such that matters, but the mutual embrace of ecclesial communities in the one apostolic faith in Christ. So we are going to be involved in a process of self-transcendence and in the reciprocal sharing of the apostolic experience. In the initial stages of reception, the Faith and Order Commission anticipates a further refinement and possible reformulation of the BEM document. But the text in this process of reformulation will have to be simultaneously transcended by the churches so that the end result will not remain an agreed statement but mutual reception and unity of the churches in love. A reciprocal openness to the quality of faith among the churches which are committed to unity is the essential context of the reception of the BEM document. I think this aspect is remarkably clear when Father Theodore says that the truth of BEM is "truth which the churches themselves are willing to recognize as apostolic truth reflecting the faith of the Church of all ages under the assumption that the Holy Spirit is missing neither from any of the great moments of Christian history nor from any of the churches of the fellowship today." If the Orthodox Churches are willing to consider for reception the BEM text, a document prepared not exclusively by Orthodox theologians, but together with Roman Catholic and Protestant theologians, as an *internal* document, that will mean the Orthodox Churches are deeply open to the quality of faith in other communities of ecclesial character and to the truth towards which the Holy Spirit leads us. The primary consideration now is not in terms of orthodoxy and heterodoxy as isolated doctrinal questions and neatly distinguished conceptual categories and propositions, but in terms of the guidance of the Holy Spirit and the unfolding of the truth in the appointed moments within the various levels and members of the Body of Christ.

Reception is an act of the whole Church, the Body of Christ. The highest authority to discern the issues of faith is the whole Body of Christ which is animated by the Holy Spirit. It is quite obvious to us that the problem with a document like BEM is that it runs the risk of remaining a theological text handled by the theologians, accepted or rejected by the visible structural authorities in the Church, without being examined by the authority of the whole Church. This is a real danger for all the churches committed to the BEM document, but especially for the Orthodox Churches because of their particular structural character. Father Theodore recognizes this fully when he emphasizes the "true consensus developed among the whole people of God" and not only "a theological convergence by theologians and church representatives alone." It is obvious that we should devise practical means of disseminating the document and inviting participatory study of it by the people at the various levels of the Church. What is of crucial importance here is the nature of ecclesial authority in the Orthodox Tradition. The BEM text offers a test for the traditional Orthodox understanding of authority as distinct from the Roman Catholic and Protestant patterns.

I think the two most important issues which are of specific concern to the Orthodox in relation to the reception of the BEM document are those of apostolic faith and Orthodox ecclesiology. Since Father Theodore has dealt with them in some detail, I will limit myself to two brief comments.

Firstly, apostolic faith is not simply a matter of the past. It seems our hearts and minds are inevitably turned to a historical past whenever we speak about the apostolic faith. If apostolic faith is only a matter of the past, then Christ to whom it bears witness is only a person of the historical past. A Church which believes in the one who has come and is to come and in the Holy Spirit who still guides us to all truth can never be chained to a few centuries of early Christianity. The dynamics of future opened by the Spirit and the Messiah who comes must be seriously taken into the very understanding of the apostolic faith. Then it becomes not only something given, but also a task, a promise and an expectation. No search for unity or reception can take off unless this vast space of freedom, promise, and possibility constantly created by the Holy Spirit is recognized in our field of ecumenical vision.

Secondly, while I fully agree with what Father Theodore says about the status of Orthodox ecclesiology in the WCC circles, I would also say that, taking into account the theological-historical context in which the World Council was originally constituted and the vast majority of the Protestant member churches which do not seem to have much concern with ecclesiology or at best consider it as one of the most peripheral of subjects, there is no immediate solution to the problem. For Orthodox Churches to stand back makes this situation only worse. Here is another test and challenge for the Orthodox Tradition. Only the quality of Orthodox witness in this matter, and no threat or complaint, can contribute positively toward the improvement of the situation. Only by our commitment to resolve the problems within the Orthodox family in line with our ecclesiological stand and by initiating a deep and extensive spiritual-theological renewal within our Churches can we be of

Tasks Facing the Orthodox in the 'Reception' Process of BEM

THOMAS HOPKO

THE WORLD COUNCIL OF CHURCHES' Faith and Order Commission statement on *Baptism, Eucharist and Ministry* presents many serious challenges to the Orthodox. These challenges have to do with the inner life and practices of the Orthodox Churches, as well as with the relationship of the Orthodox to other Christians—and to "the world"—especially within the context of the ecumenical movement. I will attempt to raise what I see to be the most compelling issues for attention, and to offer in some instances possible ways of approaching their resolution.

The Recognition of Baptisms outside the Orthodox Church

Although some members of the Orthodox Church (with many sectarians who call themselves "Orthodox") consider that all non-Orthodox Christians are not Christians at all, viewing their faith as counterfeit and their sacraments as void, if not plainly demonic, the position of the Orthodox Church over the centuries in this matter has been much more nuanced and discriminating.

While writings of Church Fathers and conciliar decrees can be cited which declare the baptism of the non-Orthodox, and their sacraments, generally, to be null and void, especially in those communities whose heretical and schismatical leaders were themselves personally once members of the orthodox, catholic Church, other Fathers and synods can also be found (sometimes involving the same Fathers and the same heretical groups) which were willing to affirm a baptismal, and so a certain sacramental and ecclesial reality, to these communities by accepting their members into Orthodox communion without baptizing (or 're-baptizing") them. (See, for example, Saint Cyprian, *Letter 70;*

Saint Athanasios, *Letter 30;* Saint Basil, *Letters 188, 199;* Laodicea Canon 8; First Constantinople, Canon 7; Second Constantinople (Trullo) 95.) This was especially true in cases involving people born into non-Orthodox communities and/or forced by circumstances to be in them against their will. (For example, see African Code Canons 48, 57, 69 concerning children baptized by Donatists; and the case of the Orthodox reception of huge numbers of uniates from Rome without baptism, chrismation or ordination of the clergy.) The issue here is not simply one of pastoral "oikonomia"—wrongly interpreted as a violation of strict ecclesiastical law and discipline. It is rather clearly an issue of spiritual discernment and theological truth.

What are we Orthodox to do today when encountering Christians of the West who have been estranged from Orthodoxy for centuries? What are we to do in this time of unprecedented theological and spiritual chaos, yet characterized by genuine theological and spiritual convergence, especially among committed praying and thinking Christian people in all traditions and confessions who are prepared to judge their communities in the light of the apostolic faith? Literally all Orthodox Churches on earth are members of the World Council of Churches, and all voted in favor of the rule that only those "churches" which confess Jesus Christ as Savior and Lord, and baptize in the name of the Holy Trinity may be members of the Council. What does such action say about the Orthodox appreciation of the baptismal, sacramental and ecclesial reality of such communities? It seems obvious to me that some sort of Christian and churchly character must be ascribed to such groups in view of the Orthodox attitude toward them in this matter. But in what way? On what basis? To what end?

If, for example, Pope John Paul II and Günther Gassmann are considered to be baptized Christians and would not be baptized (or rebaptized) should they confess the Orthodox faith and enter the communion of the Orthodox Church, what does this say, if anything, about the ecclesial character of their respective communions generally? Can any conclusion be drawn in this matter, and should it? It seems to me that Orthodox practice to date has been to evaluate and decide about the baptisms on non-Orthodox only in instances of their possible reunion with Orthodoxy. Is this so, and is it in any way relevant to the "reception" process of BEM? And how generally is the determination of the acceptability or non-acceptability of non-Orthodox baptism (and so the other sacraments) made in the first place?

The usual answer, it seems to me, to this last question has been simply to say that the Orthodox Church is prepared to discern what exists of itself outside itself, and is ready—not with reluctance, but rejoicing; not grudgingly, but with genuine gratitude—to recognize and embrace whatever is authentically "of the Church" wherever this is to be found. The difficulty obviously lay in the actual *discernment*. And it is to such discernment that we are being called in the "reception" process of BEM.

Forms of Baptism

The issue of baptismal recognition raised by BEM brings with it a particularly controversial issue now facing the Orthodox. This is the question of baptismal forms. Some Orthodox today question the reality and/or "validity" of baptisms not enacted by triple immersion in the name of the Trinity; the practice, incidentally, which the BEM section on baptism strongly recommends. While traditional Orthodox practice —scripturally prescribed, liturgically ordered and canonically legislated —is surely that of triple immersion in water in the name of the Father and the Son and the Holy Spirit, it is also the case that baptisms performed in other ways, particularly by pouring or sprinkling water, have been accepted by the Orthodox not only when done outside the canonical boundaries of the Orthodox Church, but even within them.

I myself was baptized by poured water in a church canonically within the Ecumenical Patriarchate, together with thousands, if not millions of people who were baptized this way within Orthodoxy in recent centuries in Eastern Europe and America. How is this to be taken? Are we now to be "really baptized" as some have suggested, and that after years of baptizing ourselves, and offering and receiving the holy eucharist in the Orthodox Church? Such questions must be answered for the sake of peace and unanimity within the Church, for consistency and integrity in our pastoral practices, and for justice and truth in our ecumenical relations and missionary activities.

Surely the criteria for discernment in this matter include the *faith* of the people involved, as well as the *forms* of the ritual which they use. It also involves their actual possibilities, their knowledge, their freedom and their intentions in performing the sacramental rite. It also has to do with the nature of the God in whose name the baptismal act is performed. Can we really believe, for example, that God would require the "rebaptism" of those whose intentions were pure, but whose faith and/or ritual forms were defective at the time of their original baptism? The traditional reaction of the Orthodox Church to this question, in my opinion, has clearly been negative.

Baptism, Chrismation and Eucharist

According to a number of Orthodox commentaries to BEM, the statement on baptism is considered to be at its weakest when it deals with the relationship between baptism, chrismation and holy communion. It seems to me that we Orthodox unanimously insist that two distinct rites are essential for entrance into the Church's eucharistic communion: baptism and chrismation. While avoiding scholastic nit-picking about the Spirit's role in baptism and Christ's effective presence in chrismation, we Orthodox generally relate our baptism to the death and resurrection of Jesus Christ, and our chrismation to the pentecostal coming of the Holy Spirit. We see the paschal event of baptism into Christ being fulfilled in the pentecostal sealing of the newly-baptized by God's Spirit. And we see both of these events as leading necessarily, in every instance, to eucharistic communion at the mystical supper of the Lord in the kingdom of God.

The BEM document raises several issues for us at this point. Do we consider the distinct acts of dying and rising with Christ and being sealed by God's Spirit as necessarily liturgically and sacramentally distinct, and even different? Are we prepared to identify our Orthodox chrismation with one or another form of western confirmation? Or do we see confirmation in the West as some other rite which we Orthodox do not have, which may or may not be considered as essential to apostolic faith and practice? Is this entire issue one of dogma? Or is it merely an issue of variable liturgical practices and pastoral, pedagogical action?

It seems to me, as I have already indicated, that at least in the responses to BEM which I have seen to date, the Orthodox are disposed to hold fast to the position that the initiatory rites into Church membership include baptismal rebirth, pentecostal sealing and eucharistic communion as a matter of essential, dogmatic principle; and, as such, the Orthodox are not at all prepared to recognize other practices as compatible with apostolic Christian tradition. The matter becomes further complicated when the specific issue of the eucharist is brought in.

The Orthodox Church is the only church in the last several hundred years in which all baptized and chrismated (confirmed?) people are immediately led to communion in the eucharistic supper, including infants in the care of believing adults. Some Eastern-rite Roman Catholics also follow this practice, especially since recovering their Eastern mentality and identity after Vatican Council II. And some Orthodox who were once united to Rome as Eastern-rite churches in the past still practice "first holy communion" for children reaching the "age of reason" which is usually seven or eight years of age. So again we have an issue. While tolerating ex-uniates who withhold holy communion from baptized and chrismated infants within the Orthodox Church, can the Orthodox reasonably and justly refuse to recognize, or at least to tolerate for the sake of possible recognition, such practices in others?

And if chrismation—or pentecostal sealing in some form—is insisted upon for eucharistic participation in the Orthodox Church, can the Orthodox possibly recognize as its own the practice of some Christian communions to allow, and even to defend as proper, the practice of eucharistic participation without or before confirmation—if this rite is to be considered as the western counterpart to Orthodox chrismation? And what about those who insist upon confirmation as a prerequisite for communion if, in fact, it is to be understood as something different from what the Orthodox understand by chrismation? And still further, what of those groups that have no chrismation and/or confirmation at all? Is there any hope that these communions can be viewed by the Orthodox as anything other than unacceptable? The complexity here is mind-boggling. It tempts one to think that there is no hope of formulating a position within the Church on this matter for its own sake, as well as for evaluating non-Orthodox positions and practices.

The easy way for the Orthodox would simply be to insist that no ecclesial community can be recognized as having the same faith as the Orthodox if it does not baptize, chrismate and give holy communion to all of its initiated members, including infants who are led to the mysteries by adult believers; and that the Orthodox certainly cannot recognize its own faith and life in any Christian community which in principle refuses the sacramental mysteries, including baptism itself, to qualified infants and children. In regard to baptism, Orthodox commentators on BEM unanimously denounce the practice of so-called ''believers' baptism'' as wholly unacceptable, viewing the reason for not baptizing the children of believers as solely the fear of possible apostasy in later years which would defile the sacraments of the Church as well as the soul of the initiated, and exclude the apostate from eucharistic communion in the Church for many years if not until death. But is this ''easy solution'' the right one? Can it be theoretically and practically defended by the Orthodox when some of its own canonical dioceses are themselves judged wanting by the same measure of judgment?

Baptismal Practices

The BEM document presents a special calling to the Orthodox when it speaks of baptismal practices. The Commission's call to have baptisms administered ''in the setting of the Christian community'' during ''the church's public worship,'' preferably on ''great festal occasions,'' with proper catechetical instruction for the candidates and sponsors both before and after the baptismal event, is hardly the normal practice for the Orthodox today. While social and political conditions may make such practices difficult if not outrightly impossible in some places, the fact remains that most Orthodox baptisms even in the most favorable of conditions are done privately and perfunctorily, with almost no spiritual and educational preparation and follow-up provided for the people involved, and with virtually no participation of the ecclesial community as a whole. The attempt in some Orthodox Churches in Europe and North America to have "baptismal liturgies" at which the initiatory sacraments are performed during eucharistic celebrations with the entire community assembled, usually before or during the "liturgy of the Word" has largely been met by the majority of church leaders with indifference, scepticism, fear and outright opposition and rejection. It is still the case that most Orthodox baptisms function as private ceremonies for invited guests where the celebrating minister hardly knows even the names of the people involved, and where the camera and the party are by far considered to be the most important elements in the entire operation.

The Church's Eucharistic Being

Most Orthodox to my knowledge would agree that the BEM statement on the eucharist is basically sound and remarkably adequate in its explanation of the eucharist as a sacramental rite. The hard issues at this point have to do with the application of the text to the actual faith and practices of the various churches. Most interesting for the Orthodox will be to see what the churches of the Reformation will do with this section, both in regard to eucharistic belief and eucharistic behavior. Will, for example, the document's virtual insistence that the eucharistic supper be celebrated "at least every Sunday" be received and implemented in the Protestant churches?

Two tasks surely confront the Orthodox with extreme urgency when they are faced with the BEM statement on the eucharist. One has to do with the Church's eucharistic being and life. The other has to do with the Church's eucharistic practice. Orthodox theology in our time has insisted on the eucharistic nature of the Christian Church as such. Applying the fruits of modern biblical, liturgical and patristic studies, and doing so largely in response to the demands of participation in the ecumenical movement, the Orthodox have had to explicate their understanding and experience of the Church as a mystical and divine, as well as human and historical reality within the time and space of this fallen world. The result has been the Orthodox affirmation that the one, holy, catholic and apostolic Church of Christ is fully present in its essential mystical reality when the bishop gathers with the presbyters, deacons and all the faithful people, in one place, at one time, to be filled with God's one Holy Spirit in order to attend to his one holy Word, and to eat of the one Bread and to drink of the one Cup at the one table of his kingdom at the eucharistic supper of his one Son Jesus Christ—Israel's Messiah, the Church's Bridegroom and the Lord and Savior of the world.

Thus have the Orthodox stressed the liturgical, doxological character of the Church's being and life, her sacramental and eschatological nature, her conciliar and sobornal structure. Thus, too, have the Orthodox insisted that the Church's apostolic mission in and to the world, her evangelical witness and the social and political involvement of her members, must flow from her eucharistic essence and experience, and lead back to it, as the real presence in this age of God's coming kingdom; the source and goal and content of God's eternal life already given to the faithful in fulness in the person of the glorified Christ by the action of the Holy Spirit. The proclamation has been powerful; the teaching clear; the witness firm and unyielding. But the "gap" between the *rhetoric* and the *reality* in the actual life of the Orthodox Churches has been undeniably, painfully evident—especially to those directly involved in ecumenical activity.

We Orthodox must take up the challenge of actualizing the Church as the Kingdom of God in the sacramental structures of our ecclesial communities, which means in the actual manner in which our churches, dioceses and parishes are organized and administered in this world. As it is now, we Orthodox generally appear to others, to the non-Orthodox Christians and to "the world," as a fossilized remnant of times long gone; a museum piece of long-dead dogmas and rituals, devoid of power and purpose in the contemporary world; a cluster of retarded and isolated and self-interested ghettoes of East European, Slavic, Hellenic and Semitic "ethnics" who can hardly relate to each other in a peaceful and civilized manner, not to speak of those who are not of their particular racial or religious heritage.[1] In a word, our ecclesiastical organization and activity is not formed by the eucharistic Body and Blood of Jesus Christ, but rather by the "flesh and blood" of the fallen world which, according to the apostle, "cannot inherit the kingdom" (1 Cor 15.50), nor still less bear witness to it in this present age whose "form is passing away" (1 Cor 7.21). We will speak more about this below in our section on the ministry, but for now we must see how this broad accusation applies to our present eucharistic practices.

Orthodox Eucharistic Practice Today

Contemporary eucharistic practice in the Orthodox Churches betrays

---

[1]A recent convert to the Orthodox Church writes that the common mistaken perception of Eastern Orthodoxy by western Christians is of an "unredeemably ethnic, nationalistic, sclerotic, rigid, unmoving, narrow tradition encrusted and imprisoned by the centuries, utterly lacking in life or dynamism and in a state of irreversible rigor mortis." H. Scott Trunk, "A Renunciation of the Ministry. An Anglican Goes to Orthodoxy," *The Seabury Journal,* 2, 9 (1985) 15.

not only a lack of identity between the eucharistic vision of the Scriptures and the saints on the one hand, and what is actually being done
in most places in the Church today, on the other; but it also evidences
the betrayal of what is prescribed for sacramental worship by the Orthodox Church's own service books and liturgical texts. In a discussion of BEM by Orthodox lay people in Hempstead, New York this
past winter, a woman summed up the feelings of the group when she
said that in her opinion the Orthodox ideal was the greatest and what
the Commission's statement said was wonderful, but that it appears
to her that the Orthodox Church leaders are doing everything possible
so that what ought to be done is not being done. She said that it seemed
to her as if "they put every possible obstacle in our way" when it comes
to participation in the eucharist. When pressed on the subject, and with
the help of others in the group, the following sorrowful picture was
drawn.

Orthodox Church services are long, unexplained and uninspiring.
They are conducted in a manner and language that virtually no one
can follow and understand, including the clergy who lead them, even
when this language is allegedly that of the people. The services are done
in a hurried and unengaged manner—or else are shortened in a way
that makes them misshapen and formless. Many of the prayers are read
quickly or silently or not at all, thus rendering their concluding "ex-
clamations" done aloud unintelligible and meaningless. The people are
cut off from the clergy who are physically far off, often hidden behind
a wall of icons. A choir, also often far off and hidden, sings for the
people, again frequently in a manner which renders the psalms and
hymns incomprehensible. The people stand or sit passively, watching
and listening—or dreaming, sleeping or praying their own private
prayers—as if they were attending a show. The lay people are not encouraged to receive holy communion; just the contrary. They are often
told that they do not need to partake, except during certain seasons
which are usually lenten and penitential. When they are thus urged to
participate, therefore, it is usually in an atmosphere of duty and obligation, of sin and penitence, of fear and guilt. They are ordered to fast
strictly for several days, abstaining from meat, oil and dairy products.
They are forbidden conjugal relations, except in a spirit which insinuates
that married love is generally sinful but tolerated for reproductive purposes. They are told to go to confession and to do penance, to make
prostrations and to read through many prayers. Women who are having their "time of the month" are forbidden to approach and are
often ordered not even to come to the church services, and surely not
to kiss the icons or the cross. Those who participate in communion are
then commanded to behave in a grave and serious manner befitting

the solemnity of the act. Children are not to play frivolous games. No one is to sing or laugh or dance or go to shows—not to mention whistling or spitting! Those who express the desire to receive the eucharistic gifts frequently, or even regularly on a weekly basis, which, of course would make it impossible for them to follow such a regime and to keep such rules (and so, as it is often quite seriously said, "they would only have to keep the rules for the priests"!) are considered pretentious, proud, arrogant, vain or—more benignly—overly pious, or—less benignly—dangerously fanatical. Pastors who encourage frequent and regular participation of lay people in holy communion are often labelled as themselves "fanatics," or, more usually, as "misguided innovators" who are really "Catholics" or "Protestants," having been spoiled, most likely by the ecumenical movement!

I honestly believe that this picture is not an exaggeration of the reality of the situation of the Orthodox in most places in the world today. And I believe that if something is not done about it immediately in the most forthright and courageous manner, the eucharistic life of the Church—including the proper understanding and use of liturgical worship, personal prayer, fasting, penance, sexual behavior—and generally all ascetical and devotional practices of the Christian spiritual tradition—will be discredited, disparaged and ultimately denied by the Orthodox people themselves. The fact that "other Christians" may be sinning in the opposite direction, with a lack of solemnity, reverance, spiritual discipline, and ascetical exercise in regard to eucharistic participation (not to mention apostolic faith and traditional moral behavior), is no excuse for the Orthodox to resist necessary renewal in their own Churches on the basis of their own teachings and texts. If such renewal does not occur, we Orthodox can forget about any credible witness in the ecumenical movement and any authentic missionary activity in the modern world. We can, in fact, forget about a future for Orthodoxy for the Orthodox people themselves.

Issues of Ministry

The BEM section on the Ministry appears to be the most generally problematic and unacceptable to the Orthodox. Responses thus far to this part of the document raise at least two points upon which virtually all seem to agree. One is that the ministry of bishop, presbyter and deacon in historical apostolic succession is not a negotiable issue for the Orthodox, and that no Christian body without such a ministry can possibly be fully recognized as Christ's Church. This means, practically, that Christian communities possessing—or recovering—the apostolic faith must be organically joined to the Orthodox episcopate for full recognition and communion to occur.

The second point is that the ministry of bishop and presbyter may be exercised only by men possessing certain qualifications beyond those required for baptism, chrismation and eucharistic communion in the Church; which qualifications are found clearly formulated in the Bible and the Church's liturgical and canonical tradition. Both of these issues present the Orthodox with most difficult challenges and most urgent tasks for the immediate future.

Bishop, Presbyter, and Deacon

If the Orthodox are clear about affirming the ministry of bishop, presbyter, and deacon in the Church, we are certainly not clear about the relationship of these ministries to each other, and to the ministries of all of God's people, either in past history or at the present time. How "fluid" were and are these titles and terms? What specific service is called for in these ministries? What "authority" do they possess, and how is it to be actualized in the Church (and in "the world") in a God-befitting manner? Why do the traditional scriptural and canonical qualifications exist, and what is their significance and relevance today? Is the manner in which these offices now operate in Orthodoxy, as well as the manner in which they are understood and explained in our theology, particularly in the school manuals, truly representative of authentic Orthodox theology and practice—not to mention the points made on these issues in BEM?

We Orthodox must confront these issues directly. In my opinion we have not yet formulated an adequate theology of ministry generally, and of the ordained ministries in particular. We have sources and resources in the Bible, the early Church tradition, the patristic age, the liturgy, the canons . . . but our contemporary approach to the issues at hand are still almost exclusively determined by conditions of by-gone imperial and Turkocratic times; and categories of western Reformation/Counter-Reformation debates (such as validity, power, jurisdiction, honor, authority, means of grace, which are intrinsically alien to traditional Orthodoxy). We must recover the "mind of the Fathers" on these issues, which is the mind of Christ and the mind of the Church, not only, once again, for the sake of proper and responsible participation in ecumenical activity, but for our own daily life and work in the Church without which there can be no ecumenical witness or missionary action. How, for example, can we Orthodox defend our eucharistic, doxological, conciliar, emphatically "anti-papal," "anti-Protestant" ecclesiology when in the great majority of cases our bishops function, with theological justification, as despotic autocrats answerable only to God (and perhaps to some civil authorities), but to no one else, not even each other, not to mention the people of God? And how can it be that in almost every Orthodox Church on earth the whole company of presbyters, deacons and faithful lay people are totally excluded from the process of electing, or even nominating, their bishops? Consultation in the Church is not conciliarity. And dialogues and discussion groups are not ecclesial structures for common decision making and action. Input is not *sobornost*.

The Church is hierarchical. And it is also conciliar. It is hierarchical, as Father Alexander Schmemann has written, because it is conciliar; and conciliar because it is hierarchical, in imitation of the Holy Trinity.[2] Father Alexander was not alone in his theological reflections, and he did not get them from nowhere. Karmiris, Florovsky, Popovich, Staniloae, Lossky, Meyendorff, Khodre, Nissiotis, Zizoulas, Verhovskoy, Vasileios of Stravronikita . . . and many others, in spite of all their differences and disagreements, have borne witness to the same truth on this issue. It is up to us now to develop their insights and to apply their vision to the actual organization and operation of the Churches. If we fail in our ecumenical obligations in this regard, and in our missionary duties, it will be because we have first failed in holding fast in a living way to the truth which we have received from the Lord himself within the Church "which is his body, the fulness of him who fills all in all" (Eph 1.23).

The Ministry of Women

While BEM is quiet and careful about the issue of ordaining women to the episcopate and presbyterate, there is no doubt but that the great majority of Faith and Order Commission members enthusiastically advocate such action. The WCC certainly does so as an institution, with the Orthodox being the only "confessional family" in the Council which does not ordain women to these offices and has no widespread movement calling to do so. Roman Catholics, we must remember, who have a significant number of thelogians advocating the ordination of women, are official members of the Faith and Order Commission, but are not members of the Council itself.

It is evidently of greatest urgency for us Orthodox to clarify our position about the ministry of women in the Church, about the ministry generally, both of the ordained and non-ordained members of the Church. We must find adequate words to explain why we do or do not ordain women as bishops and presbyters, and why Christians should or should not do so as a matter of principle. We also must clarify the ministry of the diaconate, determining what happened with the order

---

[2]Schmemann, A. "Toward a Theology of Councils," *Church, World, Mission,* (Crestwood, 1979), pp. 163-67.

of deaconesses in the Church, and what should be done about this order today. In this effort we must be certain to hear all voices within the Church, including those, however faint and few, who find the present Orthodox practices in this area to be questionable, and the theological reflections offered to date to be inadequate, unclear and unconvincing. And we must be careful to develop our explanations in the light of the Church's already formulated dogmas of the Trinity and the Incarnation of God's Son and Word as Jesus Christ, perfect God and perfect Man. We must come to terms with the divine names of Father, Son and Holy Spirit, as well as with the whole cadre of traditional biblical words, images, symbols and metaphors with which our theology, liturgy, church art and spiritual life literally abound. And we must deal directly with the issue of human sexuality which, I am convinced, is the crucial issue of our time—our Arianism, Nestorianism, Iconoclasm . . . —which underlies and affects contemporary thinking on all issues: God, Christ, the Spirit, the Church, the sacraments and creation itself. How we respond to the questions involving human sexuality will provide, in my view, the major criterion in times to come for evaluating the orthodoxy or heterodoxy of our theology and life.

Orthodoxia and Orthopraxia

The "reception" of BEM by all Christian communities, and surely by the Orthodox, will be ultimately one of *action* and not of thought or talk. Theologians can speak. Bishops can decree. People can discuss. But how BEM enters the lives of the Christian communities and their members, and so how BEM will contribute, or fail to contribute, to Christian unity will finally depend on what is actually done with it in the churches.

A concept often employed in ecumenical meetings which is not at all adverse to Orthodox minds is that of *orthopraxia:* right action. In ecumenical circles the word is most often applied in the area of economic, social and political activity, but it need not be confined to these issues alone. There is also *orthopraxia* in sacramental, liturgical, ministerial and ecclesial matters. The WCC Faith and Order Commission statement on *Baptism, Eucharist and Ministry* is about *orthodoxia:* right belief, right opinion and right worship. It asks the Christian churches, communions, confessional families and individual believers to consider what is right and true about baptism and holy communion and church ministry according to their understanding and experience of apostolic Christian faith and practice. But BEM is also about *orthopraxia:* right practice, right behavior and right action. It asks the churches to consider what they are actually doing when they baptize, celebrate the eucharist and exercise Christian ministry.

I am personally convinced that the "reception" of BEM by the Orthodox in the area of *orthodoxia* is relatively easy and painless. We affirm most of what is said, together with the general thrust of the document. We question whether all understand the words in the same way. We pick out several issues for pointed criticisms. And we sit back and watch what others will do. The "reception" process in terms of *ortho-praxia,* however, is in my view incomparably more difficult, painful, trying . . . and significant. Simply put, the question is whether or not we Orthodox are willing and able to let ourselves be judged by BEM in the light of our own tradition, and so to make the conscious and courageous attempt to do something about those areas of our churchly life which are out of keeping with the apostolic, and patristic, tradition of the Christian Church which we claim as our own. The point here is not about personal or corporate weaknesses and sins. The point has to do with our formal ecclesiastical life, our ecclesial structures, our very being as the Church of Christ which we confess to be the Kingdom of God sacramentally and spiritually present with us here and now within the conditions of this fallen world. The point has to do with our organization and operation as Church, our official behavior, our formal being and acting in the world. If our participation in the ecumenical movement, and in the "reception" process of BEM leads to nothing else but the purification and renewal of sacramental and spiritual life in the Orthodox Church, which necessarily means the purification and renewal of our institutional structures of church organization and administration and ministry, it will be justification enough for our ecumenical involvements and efforts over many years. And, when all is said and done, such purification and renewal may prove itself to be the single most important factor leading to the eventual "unity of all" for which the Church—and the ecumenical movement—exists, works and prays.

Response to Thomas
Hopko: "Tasks Facing the Orthodox."

METROPOLITAN CHRYSOSTOMOS OF MYRA

I COMMEND THE REVEREND PROFESSOR Hopko because in his comprehensive and succinct paper he has set before us the basic theme: that we ought not merely to give a "response" to the BEM document, thereby exercising a critique on what is correct and acceptable and what cannot possibly be acceptable from an Orthodox perspective. Rather, we must also be critical of ourselves, so much so as individual local churches as well as individuals. We must study and clarify with realism and humility those aspects of our inner life and practice which necessitate a healthy re-evaluation and re-orientation, not aiming toward something new but—as I would hope —toward that which is authentically ancient and genuinely Orthodox.

I must say that with regard to such an honest and candid position my beloved colleague finds me in agreement, at least with regards to its general outline. I congratulate him, therefore, and thank him for the paper which he has presented to us.

Professor Hopko states that BEM constitutes a serious challenge for the churches. Of course, this challenge is directed towards Orthodoxy as well. Certainly, this is the case. For this reason, even the Orthodox Churches, as the individual local Churches of the one Orthodox, are obliged—as members of the World Council of Churches (WCC)—to give a foresightful response and to offer an opinion concerning its "reception," or at least on the form and extent of this document's reception on their part.

Such is the goal of this Consultative Inter-Orthodox Symposium on Baptism, Eucharist, and Ministry; and we are grateful to all those responsible for convening it.

What, then, is the challenge of the BEM document to the Orthodox Churches?

Certain Orthodox theologians with good reason have responded to this question by speaking about repentance (*metanoia*) and by trying to determine the extent to which this *metanoia* ought to apply to us Orthodox. If we consider that self-examination and self-criticism are natural for others with regards to BEM, why ought not this apply to us Orthodox as well?

I believe that BEM offers us this twofold opportunity: 1) with the theological theses which it presents us and upon which, as a voice coming from our Tradition and traditions, we are being called upon to define our own positions; and 2) with the four questions which the authors of BEM's prologue place before the churches. We will have an opportunity to return to these two points presently.

Let us now consider more analytically Professor Hopko's positions. He states, in a categorical way, that on the fundamental issue of whether or not we accept baptism outside of Orthodoxy, there ought to be much self-examination. I agree. He says: Some Orthodox exclude baptism outside of Orthodoxy. The Church officially has followed one course on this matter, although this included many "nuanced and discriminating" elements. The fathers, on the other hand, as well as the canons and the practices of the Church present a variety of facts which are contradictory in various ways, at various times. Even "economy," which covers all things, and notably, not only "pastoral concerns," but also "the economy of ecumenism" comes forth to add recently its altered circumstances.

Examples in this instance are cases of rebaptism and reordination of particular Roman Catholics (or even of others from other confessions) coming into Orthodoxy. Several inter-ecclesiastical misunderstandings are thus created, objections from the concerned church toward the Orthodox Church are provoked, and the latter's stance is conditioned to confront the situations thus created according to the dictates of an ecumenism which is, more or less, narrowly or broadly put into practice. Thus, the issues are accommodated in each case with the desired intention that the dialogic relationship of love and theology, which has been resumed by both sides, is not disturbed. The matter is not simply an internal one confined to Orthodoxy or to its relations with Roman Catholicism. The subject is broader and is placed before us most emphatically by the BEM document.

I agree with Professor Hopko when he is so insistent as to demand that our Churches clarify their position on this subject and define the more general criteria which can possibly be maintained in this instance.

I would like at this point to refer to two specific instances from my own experience. The Pan-Orthodox Preparatory Commission in Geneva—of which I was president—investigated the question of "economy." During the first phase of its deliberations on the subjects initially placed before it, among the first and more fundamental problems set forth to which we were invited to give a pan-Orthodox response was the use of economy with regards to the recognition of the baptism of non-Orthodox; its allowable use from an Orthodox perspective in this case; the limits of this economy; and furthermore, the extent to which this economy may be used by the Church without undermining the principle of *akribeia,* given that the theology of baptism, which is the pre-eminent sacrament of Christian initiation, must be founded upon and established in an exact ecclesiology. Ours was a good attempt at that time to define the general criteria for the theology of baptism. As is known, however, this subject was excluded from the agenda of the Great and Holy Synod, and thus, a good opportunity was lost.

The second instance refers to the well-known attempt of the Orthodox Churches to have baptism in the name of the Holy Trinity recognized by the WCC as the "minimum" requirement for admittance of the churches to the WCC; that is, those churches or groups which seek admission to the WCC ought at least to believe in and practice trinitarian baptism. This suggestion of ours quite rightly provided the opportunity to posit the question to the Orthodox Churches: whether their request at the same time meant also the acceptance of baptism of the other churches and confessions, which, precisely speaking, are considered "heretical" by the Orthodox Church. You must realize what kinds of and how many difficulties we find ourselves in, as long as we do not delineate most precisely the basic criteria for the authenticity of baptism of the non-Orthodox. Professor Hopko is right in what he says concerning this.

The general criteria must be determined with regards to another subject as well: that of baptismal rites. This theme is also important and touches upon the theology of baptism. I do not believe that the issue of rebaptism today can be posited for those cases in which "ecclesial presuppositions" of the baptized, as well as of the church from which he comes, exist. Certainly, as BEM emphasizes, the more perfect rite is that of the thrice immersion and emersion. Its absence, however, and its substitution by other rites, such as those of pouring or sprinkling, do not directly raise an issue of the validity of the rite. What is of primary importance is that the ecclesial presuppositions of baptism be determined. Thus, the entire weight of Professor Hopko's paper is rightly found in paragraph five in which he speaks about the ecclesial element after which the non-Orthodox seek. I consider this need to be fundamental, and this work must be carried out with fervor on the part of the Orthodox.

I come to what my beloved colleague has said concerning the recognition of these criteria. He enumerates four criteria: the *faith* of the candidate, the *manner* of baptism, the ecclesial suppositions of the *church* from which he comes, and the *will of God*. This fourth point troubles me—not because the will of God is not of decisive importance to the entire subject of baptism and man's salvation, but because it cannot be placed on the same level of inquiry with the rest of the more external criteria found in baptism. One asks: How can we judge if the will of God is expressed in the circumstance of the candidate of this or that church? "The Spirit searches all things, even the deep things of God" (1 Cor 2.10).

In contrast, I would like to add yet another element to these criteria enumerated by Father Hopko: that of the celebrant of the sacrament. This is a most basic element which indeed plays a primary role in the recognition of the criteria of baptism's validity, and which is closely connected to the subject of baptism in relation to the priesthood.

I consider as correct all that my colleague says about the relationship between baptism, chrismation, and eucharist as well as the manner of one's admission into the eucharistic community (*koinonia*) as soon as he receives baptism and chrismation. I share his anxiety in all that he says and in the questions that he raises concerning the relationship between baptism and chrismation as well as the more profound meaning of chrismation in comparison to the *confirmatio* or the *impositio manus* of the non-Orthodox.

Of fundamental importance is his question: what will become of the one who is baptized Orthodox but who, for whatever reason, does not receive chrismation? The rubric of Orthodox practice with regard to these matters is wise. It confers these first three mysteries, all in common and together, to the one who is baptized, and naturally, to infants who have been properly guided to baptism as well. In this manner, the difficulties are alleviated. Moreover, Father Hopko's conclusions are correct (paragraph 13); namely, that a church which does not offer the three mysteries together to the candidates is not recognized as a true church, and that a church which excludes definite elements from the sacraments for particular classes of people is likewise not a true church.

I shall not give a critique here on what is stated about the "baptism of the faithful." My colleague's observations on this are correct.

However, I cannot fully agree with all that he says concerning the alteration which he claims exists today in baptism (as well as in the other sacraments which will be considered below), within the Orthodox

Church, and specifically, the manner or manners by which they are celebrated (paragraph 14). I make note of the following. Perhaps certain foreign and secular elements have been added externally. But the essence remains one and the same; the teaching moreover does not change. On these points BEM does not constitute a judgment or indictment of Orthodoxy. Rather, it must be considered an expression of the ancient Orthodox tradition, which it also seeks to restore to those churches of the West in which that tradition either does not exist or has fallen into disuse.

I now come to the subject of the eucharist. I belong to that group of theologians which considers this second edition of BEM to be less substantial than that on baptism, just as the section which pertains to the ordained ministry is weaker than either of the first two. Consequently I am in disagreement with Professor Hopko on certain of his points concerning this matter.

It is very easy for one to speculate—and this has been said by many Orthodox and Roman Catholic theologians until today—what the Protestant contigent will think and do in light of BEM's recommendation that the eucharist must be celebrated by them also every Sunday (paragraph 15). The issue is certainly not trivial. Undoubtedly, a document like BEM, when and insofar as it poses such a question to those churches, which for one reason or another, either do not have or do not preserve such a tradition, assumes a particular significance in and of itself, as well as for our Church, under the light of whose teaching we come to examine the BEM document. The text, however, raises other weak points, mainly with respect to the ordained ministry. This, indeed, must principally occupy the critic's attention.

I draw attention to paragraph 16 of Father Hopko's paper in which he describes the characteristics of the Church as eucharistic in its life and practice. I am absolutely in agreement. I do not consider, though, that those designations of eucharistic ecclesiology from an Orthodox perspective are simply *rhetorical,* and that they do not correspond to ecclesial reality. I do not think that what has been said by the fathers and is expanded upon today by all of us theologians concerning the episcopocentric eucharistic ecclesiology is hyperbolic; that it does not correspond to Orthodoxy's teaching, life, and practice. Nor do I think that the ecumenism which is exercised in Orthodoxy is detrimental to the fundamental principles of Orthodox ecclesiology.

For this reason, I cannot agree to what is stated in paragraph 18 concerning the manner in which those outside of Orthodoxy perceive us. First, they no longer see us as something static, archaic, and dead. On the contrary, there exists an intense nostalgia for Orthodoxy which necessarily passes from the contemporary expressions and leads back to the sources, about which those outside of Orthodoxy desire to know. Second, those things which can be characterized as "fossilized remnants" or as "museum pieces" are precisely those things which define the Orthodox faith in the received truth and practice of the early Church. Our innovations bring us closer to the West and toward its forms. One asks, however, what are we looking for? That we conform to the prototypes of the West in order to avoid the characterization of "fossilization," or that we bring our spiritual treasures forward so that by means of them we can attract the non-Orthodox West toward us?

In the same spirit, I do not concur with what our beloved colleague states in his lengthy paragraphs 19, 20, and 21 wherein he finds in Orthodoxy terrible antitheses between its teaching and practice, as well as many exaggerations and unacceptable conditions. I believe that all these hyperboles and anomalous circumstances do indeed refer to us. But the Church has assumed them as such within the framework of her renewing effort. Proceeding from the agenda of the Great and Holy Synod, this effort extends to the new generation of enlightened local bishops and of the analogously enlightened clergy, and moreover, is evidenced in the renewed spirit of the laity, and so the picture is other than that depicted by Father Hopko.

He will, I think, agree with me that a spirit of renewal blows within the governing Church and its individual members—one spirit which in fact differs from the Church's and its people's way of thinking that prevailed before the Second World War. This is lived daily in contemporary Orthodoxy, even in those individual local churches whose living conditions for political and societal reasons—well known to all of us—are not ideal, but on the contrary, harsh and negate any renewal. Those outside of Orthodoxy see this new spirit and recognize it today, perhaps more so and indeed more objectively than those of us who are still entangled in that familiar complex of perceiving our circumstances to be bleaker than they actually are. Indeed, as Professor Hopko states, the section on the Ministry (paragraph 22 et seq.) is the most discussed of the three that comprise the BEM document. His observation concerning the two fundamental omissions of this section is correct. He asserts the following: 1) The threefold ministry (bishop-presbyter-deacon) within the historical apostolic succession is not discussed at any length—a subject which in fact constitutes the most fundamental criterion for the recognition of any Christian body as a church; 2) the section does not refer in any way to the subject of the bishops and the presbyters possessing rights and particular characteristics, other than those conferred upon them by baptism, chrismation, and the eucharist. These rights and particular characteristics, which are applicable to them, give them the right to exercise their priestly function, as this is described and defined by the biblical, liturgical, and canonical tradition of the Church.

When these very basic themes, however, do not find a place in the pages of the BEM document, it is self-evident how difficult it is for the Orthodox Church to find its teaching and its tradition reflected in that text.

Besides this, there are also other omissions in the BEM document which are noted by Professor Hopko.

The observations and formulations which he makes in paragraph 24 are correct, and the themes which he posits are also justified. He states, and I quote: "If the Orthodox are clear about affirming the ministry of bishop, presbyter, and deacon in the Church, we are certainly not clear about the relationship of these ministries to each other, and to the ministries of all of God's people, either in past history or at the present time. How 'fluid' were and are these titles and terms? What specific service is called for in these ministries? What 'authority' do they possess, and how is it to be actualized in the Church (and in the 'world') in a God-befitting manner? Why do the traditional, scriptural and canonical qualifications exist, and what is their significance and relevance today?"

The Orthodox answer which will be given to BEM will want to underscore all those elements and to offer a precise description of the ministry and its theology in Orthodoxy. In any case, I cannot agree with what is said in paragraph 25 about the influences which the Orthodox Church's teaching encountered with regards to its priesthood and its teaching on the ministry, from the beginning, as the "theocracy" of the Byzantine years, or the degrading view of the ministry that characterized the Ottoman period ("Turkokratia") or the negative mirrorings of Reformation and Counter-Reformation prototypes upon the Orthodox clergy. Perhaps there were such influences, but it is not by chance that one pure teaching and practice concerning the ministry and the ordained priesthood was preserved in the midst of all these antithetical tensions and inclinations. This fact lives on and needs to enjoy its proper interpretation and depiction to those outside, to the non-Orthodox.

I come now to the contestable, yet extremely interesting matter, the ordination of women. This is placed in the correct perspective from what is stated initially by Professor Hopko.

Inasmuch as BEM does not speak directly about the ordination of women, nevertheless, it does raise the basic question of what their function can be within the Church. Professor Hopko also properly places the issue of "function" (*hypourgema*) which applies to all the members of the Church in general, that is to both the ordained and the non-ordained (paragraph 28). The theology on this point is of the greatest importance in and of itself, just as much as for the continuation and advancement of Orthodoxy's theological dialogues. From this perspective, too, anyone can understand that the concrete and precise formulation of the Church's teaching on this matter is one of the more fundamental responsibilities of contemporary Orthodox theology, and that it must also be expressed within the parameters of tradition, of canonical order, and of the Church's broader practice.

Even if, however, all these issues are correct and justified, and are correctly emphasized in Father Hopko's paper, I do not believe that his tendency to set the issue in terms of triadological terminology for Orthodoxy today, expecially within a perspective of human sexuality, is a correct one. If there is need of Orthodox "metanoia," this is required in many other areas, but not in those to which our colleague refers. Does he exaggerate at the end of paragraph 28 of his paper? I quote: "How we respond to the questions involving human sexuality will provide, in my view, the major criterion in times to come for evaluating the orthodoxy or heterodoxy of our theology and life."

Now I come to the last part of Professor Hopko's work where in paragraphs 29ff. he states that "the reception" of BEM by the churches will not be by thought or word, but by action, that is, by concrete decisions and analogous efforts.

Perhaps before proceeding to this point, we should clarify once more the difference between "response" and "reception."

The framework within which the churches work out every type of "response" is well known. The response is made by analyzing and critically evaluating those points in the BEM document which refer to the Church's teaching and practice with regards to three subjects under investigation: that is, baptism, eucharist, and ministry. Furthermore, the response is made by having each church clearly place on the positive or negative side certain "theses" which the document emphasizes or supports. The response is made, finally, by underscoring the degree to which the life, teaching, and practice of each church coincides with or is at a distance from the ecclesiological, sacramental, liturgical, pastoral, practical and ecumenical principles which are formulated in the document. Thus, the churches are led to answer the four basic questions found in the document's prologue. This is what the working out of the "response" means in the present instance.

In contrast, "reception" presupposes an acquisition and appropriation of the various principles presented by the document, as well as an adaptation of the teaching and practice of each church to all that is presented or suggested by the document. Naturally, "reception" cannot mean for Orthodoxy what it might mean for other churches and confessions.

BEM includes elements which the Orthodox Church, after precise theological examination, can admit as acceptable within the parameters of the "rationale" of her theology, as for example, chrismation with the holy Myron or the laying on of hands; recognition of the baptism of non-Orthodox or their rebaptism under certain circumstances; regular or frequent receiving of holy communion; the ordination of the deacon and the function of deaconesses. The Orthodox Church, however, cannot accept what is said concerning the bread and wine as being signs of the Body and Blood of Christ, or what is said about the conception of the *metousiosis* of the elements into the Body and Blood, or what is said concerning the forms of the priesthood as a functional or ordained ministry.

For the other churches, however—and here I have in mind the churches of the Reformation—"reception" means that they would recognize in practice and accept certain elements which do not exist in their traditions. These are, for example, baptism by triple immersion and emersion; chrismation in and of itself; the meaning of the three sacraments of initiation, which together enroll man into the fellowship (*koinonia*) and the kingdom of God; the change (*metabole*) of the elements into the Body and Blood of Christ; the meaning of these antitypes not as signs of remembrance of the eucharistic supper of the Savior, which occurred once, but as the elements of sacrifice offered once and for all time on behalf of our salvation; the reception of the Holy Eucharist on Sunday or even more frequently with the same fervor as currently exists in the reception by those churches of the Word through the reading and preaching of Scripture; the existence of the ordained priesthood based upon solid biblical and traditional data; and the distinction of gifts and charisms pertaining to the threefold ministry. While all these things are for the Protestant churches elements which require "reception" on their part, were they to accept the BEM document, the process of reception is different for the Orthodox. Under no circumstances can Orthodoxy be called to accept those elements which it possesses naturally, which it practices, and which in fact constitute the essence of its tradition, teaching, and practice.

This is where the meaning and content of the terms "response" and "reception" are differentiated, according to the Orthodox understanding. This point is basic for future proceedings which will follow among the individual local Orthodox Churches.

No one doubts the truth that BEM is capable of contributing to Christian unity. For this reason, I also view the document as one, absolutely positive element along this road.

All the churches have to reflect on all that the document states.

Their work will turn to the area of *orthopraxia,* as stated by Professor Hopko. But the question is will it not turn to the area of Orthodoxy as well?

I believe that these cannot be separated from one another in an absolute manner. Nevertheless, for us Orthodox, BEM will certainly be judged from the side of its orthodoxy, namely, from the perspective of Orthodoxy which it represents; and after that is done, its practical dimensions will be assessed in light of the ecclesiastical life and practice of each church.

Report

INTER-ORTHODOX SYMPOSIUM ON BAPTISM, EUCHARIST, AND MINISTRY

I. INTRODUCTION

1. WE GIVE THANKS to the triune God that we, hierarchs and theologians representing the Eastern Orthodox and Oriental Orthodox Churches, members of the World Council of Churches, were able to gather together at the Holy Cross Greek Orthodox School of Theology in Brookline, Massachusetts, USA. (A list of participants is appended to this report.) Our task was to help clarify a number of questions which might arise for the Orthodox Churches when they consider their official response to the document on *Baptism, Eucharist, and Ministry* (BEM) adopted in Lima (1982) by the Faith and Order Commission of the World Council of Churches.

2. We would like to express our gratitude to the hosts of the meeting, the Greek Orthodox Archdiocese of North and South America and the Holy Cross Greek Orthodox School of Theology, as well as to the Orthodox Task Force of the World Council of Churches and the Faith and Order Commission which made possible such a widely representative gathering. We are also grateful for the opportunity to meet with several Orthodox parishes in the Boston region.

His Eminence Archbishop Iakovos, Primate of the Greek Orthodox Archdiocese of North and South America, formally welcomed at the opening session the members of the Symposium together with other distinguished guests from the Orthodox and the other churches from the region.

3. The Moderator of the Symposium was His Eminence Prof Dr Metropolitan Chrysostomos of Myra (Ecumenical Patriarchate of Constantinople). Papers were presented on the following topics: "General Introduction on Baptism, Eucharist and Ministry in the Present

159

Ecumenical Situation" (Rev Dr Günther Gassmann, Rev Dr Gennadios Limouris); "The Meaning of Reception in Relation to Results of Ecumenical Dialogue on the Basis of BEM" (Prof Dr Nikos Nissiotis, Response: Bishop Nerses Bozabalian); "The Significance and Status of Baptism, Eucharist, and Ministry in the Ecumenical Movement" (Archbishop Kirill of Smolensk); "The BEM Document in Romanian Orthodox Theology—The Present Stage of Discussions" (Metropolitan Dr Anthony of Transylvania); "The Question of the Reception of Baptism, Eucharist, and Ministry in the Orthodox Church in the Light of its Ecumenical Commitment" (Rev Prof Dr. Theodore Stylianopoulos, Response by Rev Dr K. M. George); "Tasks Facing the Orthodox in the 'Reception Process' of Baptism, Eucharist, and Ministry" (Rev Prof Dr Thomas Hopko, Response: Metropolitan Prof Dr Chrysostomos of Myra).

4. On the basis of these papers, plenary discussions on them, and deliberations in four discussion groups, the participants in this Symposium respectfully submit the following considerations and recommendations.

II. THE SIGNIFICANCE OF BEM AND THE RESPONSIBILITY OF THE ORTHODOX

1. It appears to us that we, as Orthodox, should welcome the Lima document as an experience of a new stage in the history of the ecumenical movement. After centuries of estrangement, hostility and mutual ignorance, divided Christians are seeking to speak together on essential aspects of ecclesial life, namely baptism, eucharist, and ministry. This process is unique in terms of the wide attention which the Lima document is receiving in all the churches. We rejoice in the fact that Orthodox theologians have played a significant part in the formulation of this document.

2. In general we see BEM as a remarkable ecumenical document of doctrinal convergence. It is, therefore, to be highly commended for its serious attempt to bring to light and express today "the faith of the Church through the ages" (Preface to BEM, p. x).

3. In many sections, this faith of the Church is clearly expressed, on the basis of traditional biblical and patristic theology. There are other sections in which the Orthodox find formulations which they cannot accept and where they would wish that the effort to adhere to the faith of the Church be expressed more accurately. As often stated in the document itself, in some areas the process needs to be continued with more thinking, further deepening, and clarification.

4. Finally, there are sections in which a terminology is used which is not that to which the Orthodox are accustomed. However, in some

such cases, beneath the unfamiliar terminology, one can discover that the meaning is in fact close to the traditional faith. In other parts of BEM we notice a terminology which is familiar to the Orthodox but which can be understood in a different way.

5. We also think that the Orthodox Churches have the duty to answer responsibly the invitation of the Faith and Order Commission mainly for three reasons:

a. because here we are concerned with a matter of faith—and it has been the insistence of the Orthodox Churches for some time that the World Council of Churches should focus its attention especially on questions of faith and unity;
b. because the Orthodox have fully participated in the preparation of the text from the beginning and made a substantial contribution to it;
c. because it is important to have the response of all the Orthodox Churches, and not just some of them.

III. RESPONSE AND RECEPTION

1. Both at the Sixth General Assembly of the World Council of Churches at Vancouver (1983) and at the last meeting of the Central Committee (1984) of the WCC, the Orthodox undertook to respond to BEM as a matter of obligation and commitment with a view to furthering the ecumenical movement.

2. We would like to distinguish between the immediate response of the individual Orthodox member Churches of the World Council of Churches to the BEM document and the long-range form of the reception of the text in the Orthodox tradition. We hold that the notion of reception of the BEM document here is different from the classical Orthodox understanding of the reception of the decrees and decisions of the Holy Councils.

3. Reception of the BEM document means that we recognize in this text some of the common and constitutive elements of our faith in the matter of baptism, eucharist, and ministry so that we may stand together as far as possible to bear witness to Jesus Christ in our world and to move towards our common goal of unity. Thus reception at this stage is a step forward in the "process of our growing together in mutual trust . . . " towards doctrinal convergence and ultimately towards "communion with one another in continuity with the apostles and the teachings of the universal Church" (Preface to BEM, p. ix).

4. Reception of the BEM document as such does not necessarily imply an ecclesiological or practical recognition of the ministry and sacraments of non-Orthodox churches. Such a recognition would require a special action of the Orthodox Churches.

5. As an initial step towards this kind of reception we would wish to see official action on the part of the Orthodox Churches to facilitate the use of the BEM document for study and discussion on different levels of the Church's life so that the Church evaluates the document with a view to the ultimate unity of all churches.

6. In this process of discernment the Orthodox Churches should be sensitive to the similar process of evaluation of the text and of the process of bilateral dialogues in the member churches of the WCC and the Roman Catholic Church. Thus our evaluation will be fully informed of the ecumenical reflections and experiences stimulated by this text.

IV. SOME POINTS FOR FURTHER CLARIFICATION

1. We Orthodox recognize many positive elements in BEM which express significant aspects of the apostolic faith. Having affirmed this initial appreciation of BEM, we offer some examples among the issues which we believe need further clarification and elaboration. There are also issues which are not addressed in the text.

2. In the section on *Baptism,* we note:

a. the relationship between the unity of the Church and baptismal unity (para. 6);
b. the role of the Holy Spirit in baptism and consequently the relationship between baptism and chrismation (confirmation), linking water and the Spirit in incorporating members into the Body of Christ (para. 5, 14);
c. the role of exorcism and renunciation of the Evil One in the baptismal rite (para. 20);
d. the terms "sign," "sacramental sign," "symbol," "celebrant" (para. 22), "ethical life" and other terms throughout the text.

3. In the section on *Eucharist,* we note:

a. the relationship of the eucharist to ecclesiology in the light of the eucharistic nature of the Church and the understanding of the eucharist as "the mystery of Christ" as well as "the mystery of the Church" (para. 1);
b. the relationship between participation in the eucharist and unity of faith;
c. the role of the Holy Spirit in the eucharist, with special reference to *anamnesis* in its relation to *epiklesis* (para. 10, 12);
d. the relationship between the eucharist and repentance, confession, and reconciliation to the eucharistic congregation;
e. the meaning of sacrifice (para. 8), real presence (para. 13),

ambassador (para. 29), and the implications of "for the purpose of communion" in regard to the reservation of the eucharistic elements (para. 15);

f. the participation of baptized children in the eucharist.

4. In the section on *Ministry,* we note:

a. the link between ordained ministry today and the ministry of the apostles and apostolic succession (para. 10, 35);
b. the distinction between the priesthood of the entire people of God and the ordained priesthood, especially in light of Pauline teaching on the different functions of the members of the one Body of Christ (para. 17 & commentary);
c. issues related to the ordination of women to the priesthood (para. 18), including the way in which the problem is formulated in the text of BEM;
d. the relationship between bishop, presbyter, and deacon;
e. the relationship between *episcopé,* the bishop, and the eucharist.

V. TASKS FACING THE ORTHODOX CHURCHES

In view of future work in connection with BEM, we offer the following considerations and recommendations.

1. Steps should be taken to enable translation and distribution of the BEM document in the languages of all Orthodox Churches.

2. Orthodox Churches should see to it that the BEM document is studied and discussed in clergy and laity groups, theological faculties and seminaries, clergy associations, as well as in interconfessional groups.

3. Orthodox Churches should be open to reading BEM and to responding to it in a spirit of critical self-examination, particularly in the area of current practices in churches and parishes. They should also use this process as a stimulus and encouragement for the renewal of their life.

4. In studying and evaluating BEM, the Orthodox should move beyond the theological scholasticism of recent centuries by reappropriating the creativity and dynamics of biblical and patristic theology. This will enable them to move towards broader perspectives and to think more deeply about certain issues.

5. In their ongoing bilateral conversation, Orthodox Churches should take BEM into account.

VI. PERSPECTIVES FOR FUTURE FAITH AND ORDER WORK

In view of the future work of the Faith and Order Commission and the WCC as a whole, we recommend the following perspectives for a proper interrelationship between BEM and the Faith and Order study projects "Towards the Common Expression of the Apostolic Faith Today" and "The Unity of the Church and the Renewal of Human Community."

1. The process of an ecumenical reappropriation of the apostolic faith and tradition as it was begun in the BEM document should be consciously continued in the two other study projects.

2. There should be a clear understanding that baptism, eucharist, and ministry are essential elements of the apostolic faith and tradition. At the same time, they are fundamental expressions of the witness and service of the Church for today's world and its needs, its concerns, and its renewal. Renewal of both the life of the Church and of the world cannot be separated from the liturgical and the sacramental life of the Church nor from its pastoral responsibility.

3. These two other projects should also be open to insights and suggestions expressed in the responses of the churches to BEM and profit from them.

4. The Lima document highlights the important relationship between the "rule of faith" and the "rule of prayer," to which the Orthodox are so deeply committed. Therefore, we hope that in the two other study projects of Faith and Order this significant insight is seriously taken into account as well.

5. We further recommend that one important point in future work of the Faith and Order Commission in relationship to BEM should be the clarification of theological terminology and of linguistic problems in translation. This seems to be necessary in view of the heading "Ministry" of the third section of BEM and terms such as "sign," "reception," and "believer's/adult baptism."

6. Starting from a clarification of the vision of the Church which undergirds BEM, the future work of Faith and Order should concentrate on ecclesiology by bringing together the ecclesiological perspectives in BEM, in the responses of the churches to BEM, and in the other study projects of Faith and Order.

* * * * *

We, the participants in the Symposium, experienced this meeting as an occasion for exchanging our views and clarifying common perspectives. We saw in it also an important means for furthering contacts and cooperation among the Orthodox Churches and thereby promoting our conciliar spirit.

List of Participants

INTER-ORTHODOX SYMPOSIUM ON BAPTISM, EUCHARIST, AND MINISTRY

Host: Archbishop Iakovos, Primate of the Greek Orthodox Arch-diocese of North and South America, Exarch of the Ecumenical Patriarchate, 10 East 79th Street, New York, NY 11021, USA

PARTICIPANTS FROM MEMBER CHURCHES OF WCC

Metropolitan Prof Dr Chrysostomos of Myra (Ecumenical Patriar-chate of Constantinople), P.O. Box 1225, Sirkeçi, Istanbul, Turkey

Metropolitan Parthenios of Carthage (Greek Orthodox Patriarchate of Alexandria), Cardeadou Street 37, 106 76 Athens, Greece

Rev Prof Paul Tarazi (Greek Orthodox Patriarchate of Antioch), St. Vladimir's Seminary, 575 Scarsdale Road, Crestwood, NY 10707, USA

Prof Dr George Galitis (Greek Orthodox Patriarchate of Jerusalem), 4, Sechou Street, 115 24 Athens, Greece

Archbishop Kirill of Smolensk and Vysma (Russian Orthodox Church), 18/2 Ryleeva, 121 002 Moscow, USSR

Rev Prof Dr Athanassios Yevtič (Serbian Orthodox Church), Faculty of the Serbian Orthodox Church, u. 7 Jula br. 2, 111 00 Belgrade, Yugoslavia

Metropolitan Dr Anthony of Transylvania (Romanian Orthodox Church), Str. 1 Mai 24, 2400 Sibiu, Romania

Mgr Joseph, Bishop of Velyka (Bulgarian Orthodox Church), 1953 Stockbridge Road, Akron, Ohio 44313, USA

Dr Benedictos Englezakis (Church of Cyprus), P.O. Box 1130, Nicosia, Cyprus

Metropolitan Prof Dr Chrysostomos of Peristerion (Church of Greece), P. Tsaldaris, 63, Peristeri, Athens, Greece

Bishop Jeremias of Wrocaw & Szczecin (Polish Orthodox Autocephalic Church), Al. Gen. K. Swierczewskego 53, 03 402 Warsaw, Poland

Rev Fr Ambrosius (Finnish Orthodox Church), Valamo Monastery, 79850 Uusi-Valamo, Finland

Archpriest Dr Jaroslav Suvarsky (Orthodox Church of Czechoslavakia), V. Jame 6, 111 1 Praha 1, CSSR

Rev Leonid Kishkovsky (Orthodox Church in America), P.O. Box 675, Syosset, NY 11791, USA

Bishop Nerses Bozabalian (Armenian Apostolic Church, Etchmiadzin), Catholicosate, Holy See of Etchmiadzin, Armenian SSR

Bishop Bishoi of Damietta (Coptic Orthodox Church), Anba Rueis Bldg., P.O. Box 9035, Nasr City, Cairo, Egypt

Archbishop Gregorios of Shoa (Ethiopian Orthodox Church), P.O. Box 1283, Addis Ababa, Ethiopia

Archbishop Mesrob Ashjian (Armenian Apostolic Church), 138 East 39th Street, New York, NY 10016, USA

Rev Dr K. M. George (Orthodox Syrian Church of the East), Orthodox Theological Seminary, P.O. Box 98, Kottayam, Kerala 686.001, India

THEOLOGICAL SCHOOLS

Prof Dr (Mrs.) Nikolitsa Nikolakakou, Department of Pastoral Theology, University of Athens, Strateg. Makrygianni 23, 15772 Zographos/Athens, Greece

Prof Konstantinos Skouteris, Department of Theology, University of Athens, University Campus, Ano Ilisia, Athens, Greece

Prof Dr Ioannis Anastassiou, Department of Theology, University of Thessalonike, Prigipos Nikolaou Str. 16, 546 22 Thessalonike, Greece

Prof Dr Nicholas Lossky, St. Sergius Orthodox Theological Institute, 66, rue d'Hautpoul, 75019 Paris, France

Rev Prof Dr Alkiviadis Calivas, Dean, Holy Cross Greek Orthodox School of Theology, 50 Goddard Avenue, Brookline, MA 02146, USA

Rev Prof Dr Thomas Hopko, St. Vladimir's Seminary, 575 Scarsdale Road, Crestwood, NY 10707, USA

ADVISERS

Prof Dr Nikos Nissiotis, Dean, Department of Pastoral Theology, University of Athens, University Campus, Ano Ilisia, Athens, Greece

Dr Alexandros Papaderos, Director, Orthodox Academy of Crete, 73006 Kolympari, Chania, Crete, Greece

Prof (Mrs.) Catherina Chiotellis (Center of Translation and Interpretation in Corfu), 100, Vouliagmenis Street, 11743 Athens, Greece

Rev Dr David Burke, Lutheran World Ministries, Lutheran Center, 360 Park Avenue South, New York, NY 10010, USA

Rev Fr John Long, SJ, National Conference of Catholic Bishops, 2502 Belmont Avenue, Bronx, NY 10458, USA

Guest: Metropolitan Emilianos of Sylivria (Ecumenical Patriarchate), 11 Avenue Riant-Parc, 1200 Geneva, Switzerland

OTHER PARTICIPANTS FROM THE UNITED STATES

Rev Dr Robert G. Stephanopoulos (Dean of Holy Trinity Greek Orthodox Archdiocesan Cathedral), 319 East 74th Street, New York, NY 10021, USA

Prof Dr George Bebis (Holy Cross Greek Orthodox School of Theology), 50 Goddard Avenue, Brookline, MA 02146, USA

Bishop Prof Dr Demetrios of Vresthena (Holy Cross Greek Orthodox School of Theology), 50 Goddard Avenue, Brookline, MA 02146, USA

Rev Prof Thomas FitzGerald (Holy Cross Greek Orthodox School of Theology), 50 Goddard Avenue, Brookline, MA 02146, USA

Rev Prof Dr John Travis (Holy Cross Greek Orthodox School of Theology), 50 Goddard Avenue, Brookline, MA 02146, USA

Prof Dr Kyriaki A. FitzGerald (Holy Cross Greek Orthodox School of Theology), 50 Goddard Avenue, Brookline, MA 02146, USA

Ms. Elaine Alexis Gounaris (Ecumenical Office of Greek Orthodox Archdiocese), 10 East 79th Street, New York, NY 10029, USA

Archpriest Sergiy Suzdalstsev (Dean of the Russian Orthodox Cathedral of St. Nicholas), 15 East 97th Street, New York, NY 10029, USA

Rev Fr George Corey (Orthodox Church in America), St. George Church, 55 Emmonsdale Road, P.O. Box 164, Boston, MA 02132-0164, USA

Mrs. Susan Arida (Orthodox Church in America), 1 Auburn Court, Brookline, MA 02116, USA

Ms. Constance Tarasar (St. Vladimir's Seminary), 575 Scarsdale Road, Crestwood, NY 10707, USA

Rev Fr Yeprem Kelegian (Armenian Apostolic Church, Etchmiadzin), Armenian Church, 630 Second Avenue, New York, NY USA

WCC STAFF (150, route de Ferney, 1211 Geneva 20, Switzerland)

Rev Prof Ion Bria, Moderator of Orthodox Task Force

Rev Dr Emilio Castro, General Secretary of WCC (June 12 only)

Rev Dr Günther Gassmann, Director of the Faith and Order Secretariat

Rev Dr Gennadios Limouris, Executive Secretary, Faith and Order Secretariat

G. Protopresbyter George Tsetsis, Representative of Ecumenical Patriarchate of Constantinople

Ms. Carol Thysell, National Council of Churches, Faith and Order Commission (secretarial assistance)

Mr Mstislav Voskressensky, Russian Orthodox Church (interpreter)

HELLENIC COLLEGE/HOLY CROSS PRESS

SAINT SYMEON OF THESSALONIKE
A TREATISE ON PRAYER
Trans. H. L. Simmons

A Treatise on Prayer is an important Byzantine liturgical and historical source. In this study, Symeon explains the meaning and significance of what happens and is said in the services of the Orthodox Church in the fifteenth century.

ISBN 0-917653-05-4 $6.95 paperbound
ISBN 0-917653-06-8 $11.95 clothbound

* * * * * * * * * * * *

ROME AND CONSTANTINOPLE
Essays in the Dialogue of Love
Edited by Robert Barringer

This collection of essays is a product of the Saints Peter and Andrew Lectures, a forum for practical and theological exchange between Roman Catholics and Orthodox Christians. It contains four essays which address historical, spiritual, ecumenical, and theological issues.

ISBN 0-917651-04-09 $4.95 paperbound

* * * * * * * * * * * *

BYZANTINE HYMNOGRAPHY
and
BYZANTINE CHANT
by Dimitri Conomos

Professor Dimitri Conomos, one of the leading Byzantine musicologists, was chosen to inaugurate the "Nicholas E. Kulukundis Lectures in the History of Hellenism" at Hellenic College/Holy Cross School of Theology. In the first presentation, the author offers us a concise, brilliant survey of Byzantine hymnography—"the poetical expression of Orthodox theology, translated through music to the sphere of devotion." In the second, Dr. Conomos discusses the development of Byzantine music . . . "the medieval sacred chant of all Christian churches following the Eastern Orthodox rite."

ISBN 0-917653-04-1 $4.95 paperbound

THE LIFE OF SAINT NICHOLAS OF SION
By Ihor and Nancy Ševčenko

The authors offer the text, translation and commentary of the life of St. Nicholas, Abbot of the Monastery of Holy Sion near Myra in Lycia (Asia Minor).

The Life, written soon after the saint's death (c.564), contributed to the growth of the more famous Life of St. Nicholas of Myra.

The book is important for the information it offers on the history and geography of Lycia, and the down-to-earth piety of the sixth-century Christian world. The volume includes sixteen illustrations, five of which appear for the first time.

ISBN 0-917653-02-5 $15.95 clothbound
ISBN 0-917653-03-3 $9.95 paperbound

Errata

Page 48, line 12: for thorugh—read,   thorough

Page 50, line 22: for exxceptional—read,   exceptional

Page 56, line 3: for Catholiocs—read,   Catholics

Page 85, line 9: for Counterreformation—read,   Counter-Reformation

Page 109, line 11: for George Florovsky—read,   Georges Florovsky

Page 129, line 13: for Orthodox churches—read,   Orthodox Churches